2004

Ms. Baba –

Haven't we howled
up a storm!

For me a great
privilege!

All the best,

Dr. Katz

HOWLING WITH SAKUTARÔ

What do you get when an irreverent, deep-thinking, passionate psychoanalyst crosses swords with a Japanese poet and mixes up the conversational process by way of Sigmund Freud, Melanie Klein and Wilfred Bion? Why, nothing less than the provocative and engrossing *Howling with Sakutarô*, a paean to the artistry of the unconscious.

Donna Perlmutter,
author of *Shadowplay: The Life of Antony Tudor*

You will enjoy Kurth's unusual exposition and at times wonder whether it is Sakutarô or "you" that is the real subject. So treat yourself to a bit of well-explained psychoanalysis."

Armen A. Alchian
Professor of Economics, UCLA

Kurth's tour de force places Hagiwara Sakutarô (1886-1942) on the psychoanalytical couch in a series of analytical encounters that break new ground in how analysis can be used to deal with creative artists beyond our times. Utilizing Robert Epp's meticulous and sensitive translations of Hagiwara's poetry, Kurth is able to bring to life the inner dynamics of Hagiwara's personality and the source of his sensuous poetic inspiration. This is a work that bridges East and West and reveals to us the common human ties that transcend race and culture.

Fred G. Notehelfer
Professor of Japanese History
Director, UCLA Center for Japanese Studies

The imaginary encounter of a psychoanalyst with Japan's greatest modern poet is a revealing therapeutic drama, an engaging display of insights into his poetry, and, not coincidentally, in its quotations and biographical notes, testimony to the meticulous devotion of Hagiwara Sakutarô's translator. The fashionable biases against translation, biography, and the "talking cure" are effectively challenged in a thoroughly delightful way.

Howard Hibbett, Victor S. Thomas Professor of Japanese Literature,
Emeritus, Harvard University

HOWLING
WITH
SAKUTARÔ

Cries of a Cosmic Waif

by Frederick Kurth

Translations and Annotations by Robert C. Epp

www.zamazamapress.com

2004

Frederick Kurth, M. D., Indiana University School of Medicine, 1955

Translations and Annotations by Robert C. Epp, Professor Emeritus, UCLA.

ZamaZama Press
3109 Colby Avenue
Los Angeles, CA 90066
www.zamazamapress.com
Printed in the United States of America

ISBN: 0-9746714-2-8

First Edition
1 2 3 4 5 6 7 8 9

Library of Congress Cataloging-in-Publication Data

Editing and book design by Thema www.thema.us
Cover illustration and design and interior illustrations by Maureen Burdock. Crow icon in session headers is taken from the cover of a work of Hagiwara Sakutarô published in 1929.

To Wilfred and Ken

CONTENTS

ACKNOWLEDGEMENTS

An invoicing of the debts I owe would go back to my Cro-Magnon relatives some 50,000 years ago. They brought about the Great Leap Forward by leaping on that qualitative emergent we call symbolic language. It marked the beginning of ZamaZama. Alas, if I went back to the beginning, I'd never get to Sakutarô in this lifetime.

Dr. Robert Epp spent a good chunk of thirty years working with Sakutarô. He sent me *Rats' Nests* five years ago, beginning an astonishing journey. In Bob's translations, the unadorned and brutal nakedness of Sakutarô's writing howls off the page. The work of a great poet links fresh figures with unprecedented thoughts, and that's exactly what Sakutarô and Bob pull off. Bob insists he's nothing but a "beaver," scholarly, exhaustive, careful. He is also a great artist. Every line of Sakutarô he transforms into plain, living, wonderful English. I don't know a word of Japanese, but I know that's the kind of writing Sakutarô intended. Put simply, Bob translates world class writing into world class writing.

Rhonda Winchell Sharp "re-flowed" this book. Serving as a magnificent hostess, she set the table for Sakutarô and me, and then she had Freud and Melanie and Wilfred join us.

Simon Levy, a theater man for all seasons, knows how to tell a story. His unerring sense of what is alive infuses every step of Sakutarô's astonishing journey as told in these conversations. Simon read through the book twice, line by line. Nothing got by his insistence on pace, focus and verve.

You need only glance at Mr. Crow on the cover to recognize Maureen Burdock's immense gift. "I'm a nihilistic crow," Sakutarô exults, wonderfully sassy. Cynthia Green made many a textual rough place smooth. Astonishingly, in Session 36 she hammered on me until the complexities of Sakutarô, Bion and Spengler got transformed into thrilling transparency.

When I started psychoanalysis with Ken Beach in 1955, I spoke like a theologian. Ken was the chief conspirator who masterminded my escape from a theological tutelage. From him I learned to talk like an ordinary human being.

READER'S GUIDE

Howling with Sakutarô consists of thirty-six imaginary conversations between psychoanalyst Frederick Kurth and Hagiwara Sakutarô, the father of modern Japanese poetry (1886-1942). The discussions cover nearly twenty years of Sakutarô's life.

Each chapter is divided into two subheadings:

"Notes from Underground" present imagined conversational interchanges between Fred and the poet. Sakutarô's contributions to the dialogues consist entirely of lines extracted from his published work and are presented in bold face throughout the book.

"Notes from Aboveground" present historical and cultural details from Sakutarô's life and work. These remarks have been adapted from annotations in *Rats' Nests* (Paris: UNESCO Publishing, 1999).

INTRODUCTION

All of us are great communicators. An essential need of every human is to tell stories. Stories. Stories. Stories. Morning till night. As toddlers. In our dotage. Stories cohere. They have a beginning, a middle and an end. Our lives keep going to pieces, but a story puts the pieces back together again. Stories center us and keep us from wobbling off the planet. Throughout this book, our ferocious compulsion to talk will be called ZamaZama.

A problem is that we ask our stories only to be plausible. They don't have to be true. In fact, plausibility is a great enemy of truth. From the stories told to him in his consultation room, Freud could have indicted plausibly the entire population of Vienna. Again and again, patients shocked him with tales of childhood seductions. Hardly surprising that in 1897, when he strolled Vienna after his day's work, greeting passers-by with impeccable civility, Freud found himself mightily confused. Was he to conclude that the courteous and refined citizens also out taking the air of his beloved Vienna were secretly sexually deranged? Was that possible?

Freud decided the only way to clarify this disturbing conundrum was to go into the story-telling business himself. He called his story, "A Self-Analysis." On the basis of his dreams and free associations, he set out to discover the workings of his mind and to find out what lurked there. His story established the whole field of talking therapies and made him world renowned.

Meanwhile, on the other side of the planet, about the same time, Hagiwara Sakutarô decided he'd do something very similar. A Japanese literary artist and, later, national icon, Sakutarô set out to unravel the workings of his mind through the free productions of his writings. His story made him also world renowned. Both these systematic raconteurs came up with a wildly implausible tale, namely, that a secret to understanding sexual life lies in the minds of the infant, toddler and child. Previously, the race had assumed sexuality begins with puberty. As Freud told his story, relentlessly and unflinchingly, the truth proved counter-intuitive. Sexual life does not begin with puberty but at our very birth.

Primarily through his self-analysis, Freud came to appreciate the enormous complexity of what he called "infantile sexuality." Simply put, he learned that children are people with complicated feelings and interior lives. Children should be seen and children should be heard, for what transpires in those formative years shapes a personality decisively.

Sakutarô tells a story also wildly implausible but astonishingly similar to the one related by Freud. Of course, neither man knew he was partnered in his shocking ZamaZama with a fellow communicator ten thousand miles away.

Freud went on to work out a systematic procedure for examining how human beings think and feel and act. That procedure is psychoanalysis, a method of sharing one's story with another person in order to bring it vividly to life.

Freud's work was carried forward by thousands of colleagues, most notably by Melanie Klein and Wilfred Bion, and, most humbly, myself. I had the great good fortune to work personally with Wilfred for ten years. He in turn had undergone psychoanalysis with Melanie, who had worked directly with Freud.

Melanie Klein, without much formal education, initiated her career by working in Sandor Ferenzi's Budapest Clinic at the end of World War I. Ferenzi played a major role in the development of psychoanalysis. Klein moved to England in 1926 where she made momentous contributions, such as greatly deepening play therapy as a tool for investigating the mind of the child. Melanie explored the life-creating bond between mother and child, an infant's do-or-die relationship with The Breast. Experienced as benign, The Breast evokes life-giving gratitude and the living of one's years as an incomparable gift. Melanie is a wonder, telling stories she overheard in the minds of young children that, like Hamlet's ghost, cause "knotted and combined locks to part/And each particular hair to stand on end." Melanie discovered our deepest attachment, that to The Breast, is endlessly threatened by envy, the green-eyed monster that stalks the human world like a marauding Grendel. Melanie never flinched. She possessed a "Third Ear," exactly attuned to the importunate cries of young children.

I first met Wilfred Bion when I told him a "story" I was experiencing with a conversational partner undergoing psychoanalysis with me. Bion was born of British parents in India and returned to his home country at age eight. He served in World War I as a tank commander, receiving the highest decoration of the British government for bravery. Wilfred spent the last ten years of his professional life in Los Angeles.

Bion made major contributions to psychoanalysis, building on Freud and Klein's work. He recognized mind as a human creation, a tool whose chief work is to deal with the internal world by developing the power to think "unthinkable thoughts." For example, an infant experiences hunger as life-threatening: "I am dying." Klein demonstrated that the infant projects this terror into The Breast where it can be detoxified and thereby made useful for learning: "I am not dying. The Breast protects me." Bion recognized that this first human experience forms the basis for the speaker-hearer relationship, one based on symbolic language. In his "Grid" he detailed how language gets shaped into an ever more sophisticated tool for thinking thoughts, beginning with what Bion called the acquisition of alpha-function, a capacity to transform experiences into living language enabling the work of mind. However, thinking in the vortex of emotional life presents an extraordinarily difficult assignment.

When I finished telling Bion my partner's story, Wilfred said nothing. We sat together in perfect silence. For twenty minutes. It seemed like forever. Finally Wilfred said, "It'll be a long analysis." It took me a year to realize he had brought that aspect of the story vividly to life in his "supervision." Wilfred had an unfailing sense of what is alive. He understood that experience has to come before knowledge. You have to live the story to learn anything truly useful from the experience.

I've invited Sakutarô to tell me his story. He and I engage in thirty-six sessions vivifying the timeless elements in his life. Sakutarô's responses are based on his literary work. I add nothing to his published statements, responding to them conversationally. I use little biographical data, as is my practice with every partner, focusing almost exclusively on what transpires between the two of us.

We all know every computer houses programming languages which have rigid notions of syntax. We may not know that another program also exists within each computer called a "compiler." The compiler parses a programming language and provides instructions that its central processing unit can execute.

One can think of Sakutarô's writings as a "program" for a compiler or interpreter that hadn't been invented yet. Sakutarô wanted his writings to express the life of the mind. He began this undertaking by making a major break with the rigid literary tradition which had existed in Japan for the previous one thousand years. He determined that this tradition would not allow him to achieve his objective, so he turned to free verse. He still lacked a compiler. Remarkably, at that very time, on the other side of the globe, Freud was busily creating such a tool.

The language of psychoanalysis is conversation, a very free-flowing language, instructed by a compiler very different from the traditional one used by Japanese writers for a millennium. Sakutarô's use of free verse generates a language much more like everyday conversation.

However momentous this huge step taken by Sakutarô, he still lacked an effective compiler, not for creating literature, but for interpreting his works in a way that would reveal the workings of mind. Such an instrument is what Freud and Klein and Bion and many others hammered out over the last one hundred years, and its astonishing power is what I intend to demonstrate in the following conversations.

Remarkably, Wilfred introduced me to the concept of a compiler. I was telling him about a conversational partner who was a world class scholar and spoke ten languages. Alas, I told Wilfred, "He speaks psychotic." Wilfred replied, "Maybe so, but not in ten languages."

It is important to note that the psychoanalytic compiler has to do with conversation, not literature. I am adding nothing to Sakutarô's work as an artist. The analytic compiler is useful only for the ordinary human being. Not taking anything away from their genius, both Freud and Sakutarô were ordinary people. What Sakutarô lacked is similar to what Darwin lacked. Darwin desperately needed Mendel's compiler. Mendel's peas revealed discrete and permanent heritable entities that prevented "melding" of traits, thus providing natural selection something to select from. Darwin never knew of Mendel's work, while carrying out his own work at exactly the same time, since Mendel was "over there, just across the channel." Darwin had no doubt that genes—or whatever they might be called—would come along someday even as Sakutarô assumed the same for psychoanalysis.

The use of the couch is designed to take eye contact out of the speaker-hearer relationship. That's its only function, but this is important. Words serve marvelously to illuminate the internal domain, and the intensity of visual communication easily compromises that focus. When printed in verse form, the literary structure acts as a wall on the page, again interfering with conversational flow, so I print Sakutarô's free verse as prose. The very magnificence of Sakutarô's language, its cadences and literary glories, are an unintended enrichment and joy, but I have other fish to fry.

Great communicators like all of us have many compilers, but in this scientific effort I select only a particular one for our attention. Much of what a speaker says from the point of view of the psychoanalytic compiler is defensive in nature, obfuscating, evasive, an inevitable consequence of needing to avoid pain. When something "psychoanalytic" breaks through, that is what I then select. However, the poems referenced in the sessions—even if only one line—are noted in the appendix, session by session seriatim. I provide the page number where each poem appears in Dr. Robert Epp's *Rats' Nests* (Paris: UNESCO Publishing, 1999).

Dr. Epp spent thirty years translating Sakutarô into conversational English. Epp, too, is a wonder. "Get me the plain syntax of everyday speech," Sakutarô seems to demand. "I want to speak truthfully and plainly about me." Epp provides biographical notes on Sakutarô at the end of each conversation which I call "Notes from Aboveground."

Critics complain that Freud's cases read like novels. They dismiss him as merely a humanist or philosopher. Or a mere storyteller. Precisely! That's his genius. The mind is structured out of paradox. We use finite resources like vocabulary and rules of syntax to create an instrument limitless in its power and sweep. Language makes possible the telling of stories, with a beginning and end, finite in their themes and plots, but as infinite as personal knowledge and as unendingly unique as human beings.

In *Howling with Sakutarô* Hagiwara Sakutarô and I will be telling a story within a story. Does a life in the little town of Maebashi, Japan, a hundred years ago, demonstrate the same issues and struggles as a life in Freud's Vienna, Melanie's London, and Wilfred's Los Angeles? Do Sakutarô's struggles with his life as he experienced sex, love, family, religion, mind and brain problems, group issues, and God, speak to everyone? Does his journey from a closed world to an infinite universe make cosmic waifs of all of us?

The final story within the story is mine and, I hope, yours.

Across half our world and time, Sakutarô howls, "That's ZamaZama!"

Hagiwara Sakutarô, 1915–1916

PART I

Agonizing Revelations

NOTES FROM UNDERGROUND

Hagiwara Sakutarô arrives on time. I open the door to my waiting room. He is wearing a snazzy suit, with spats no less. He brandishes a fine cane and wears a red-tasseled Turkish fez. I can't help myself. I break out in a broad smile. A small man, wiry and intense, his eyes radiate intelligence.

Walking in without further ado, Sakutarô seats himself comfortably in a chair. He keeps on his fez. Sakutarô says he spends his life trying to understand himself through writing, what he thinks of as "a living, active psychology," reflecting the natural workings of his mind. He read a bit of Freud but found him remote. However, when his translator, Robert Epp, suggested perhaps personal psychoanalysis could help him in his life's quest, he decided to look me up. Thus he appears, and I offer to see him twice a week. This surprises him. He read that undergoing psychoanalysis requires sessions five times a week.

"Those days psychoanalysis still fostered a numerology," I answer. I spell out issues of time and money. Whether he shows up for his sessions or not is his responsibility. Until he fires me, however, I expect to be paid for the ones he misses. Since I am not in the banking business, I also expect to be paid the first session of each month. He seems completely disinterested in these details, patting his fez several times and glancing about the room. He asks when we could start. "We already have," I reply. He asks about using the couch. "That's up to you. I have no idea whether you'd find the couch useful."

He gets up and walks to it. While patting it, he eyes me and then sits down on it. I move to my chair at the head of the couch. He looks at me, seeming puzzled and not knowing exactly what to make of it all.

He keeps staring at me and says straightforward,

On my way home from a stroll, tepid afternoon sunlight drifted over my sweaty cuffs as growing hunger lit fireworks in me. Exhilarated, I went to the second floor of the steakhouse and gaped spellbound at passing trams.

I say, "I think you find starting this work is like starting a journey. Exhilarating and at the moment has you spellbound." Sakutarô looks at me as though thunderstruck. This happens often in my lab.

I continue, "You raise an interesting puzzle, experiencing hunger as vivid as fireworks. Sensibly enough, you go to the second floor of a steakhouse, but instead of eating, you gape at passing trams."

Sakutarô seems ready to bolt. Not surprising. Conversational partners often experience a mere observation as a Jovian thunderbolt, something Freud noted with amazement when he first began this work. Sakutarô looks away. Then, to my surprise, he takes off his fez and places it on the carpet. Holding on to his cane, he lies down on the couch and says,

I roamed the banks of the Toné yesterday, planning again to throw myself in, but the current ran too swift. Unable to stem my griefs, I swallowed all shame and stayed with life.

"Instead of throwing yourself into the river, you threw yourself into your writing. Just now you threw yourself on to the couch. So far you're staying with life."

I dote on my useless self. Who would drown a pitiful fellow like me? Best to indulge myself and weep.

He twirls his cane in the air while straining to turn his head around far enough so he can see my face and adds,

To be truthful, whatever I do tears are my life.

His tone is supercilious, almost mocking. I tilt my head so that I am looking squarely back at him. "I think what you're saying is exactly the truth, and it's all but killing you."

He snaps his head back, shaking it as though he has just experienced a blow and whispers,

Although I no longer spend my days yearning for her with my whole being, mine was such a love nothing can stem my tears.

Immediately he shakes himself again and says flatly,

Last night I stole some money. The truth is I had been drinking a bit.

Sakutarô vividly describes purloining a five-yen note from his mother's cabinet, allowing himself the histrionics of impersonating a great thief.

The truth is I had been drinking a bit. I now found my friends repulsive. Beautiful women I regarded my foes. I felt like doing them all in. Everything law-abiding in my heart schemed revolt.

From tears to violence in nothing flat. He turns contemptuous and mocking.

Biting my lips, I thought of the shame and agonies of confession. After all, since I'm a poet and an atheist, as well, I wouldn't think of asking forgiveness either from a friend or from Jesus.

"Forgiveness?" I query. He goes on as though I hadn't spoken a word.

When I took the money...

He stops and takes a deep breath.

Mother is my goddess.

Again he pauses. When he resumes, he speaks in measured cadence.

Daybreak's dim light chills finger smudges on the windows. Faintly whitening mountain ridges lie serene as mercury.

"You speak as a poet."

Other passengers are still asleep. The saccharin stench of varnish and whiffs of lingering cigar smoke on this night train distress my wasted tongue.

A tear rolls down his cheek.

How must they disquiet my married friend! "Haven't we passed Yamashina yet?" she asks. With feminine tact she then deflates her just-unplugged air pillow. Snuggling together in grief near dawn, we glance aimlessly out the window.

The tears now tumble down his face.

Though tears of grief flow in endless torrents, my agonies do not dissolve. It's truly impossible to abandon one's dreams, but this of all my dreams I cannot let go. I'm totally devastated, my heart shredded. I can't help crying out: Return my love to me—return her now!

Bolting into a sitting position, Sakutarô scares the bejesus out of me. He glares straight ahead, his cane at the ready.

Keep away from women. Don't chase after and moon over them. Don't flatter a woman, hold her hand, praise her features, or curry her favor. Women are sacred idols. But keep away from women, for you cannot comprehend them. Hold in contempt and disdain those who pursue women.

Sneering, Sakutarô looks at me.

Such lowlifes as Byron and Heine, for example, fellows constantly chasing after and mooning over them—poets who specialize in seduction. Never lay a hand on a woman.

Simply gaze at her solemn essence from afar.

Sakutarô keeps staring at me, defiant. I feel exhilarated. Challenged. "If I may paraphrase another writer—when idealization comes, can persecution be far behind? You tell us your mother is a goddess. You tell us you cannot go on without the love of your married friend. And then, Boom! you warn us to keep away from women."

The life seems to go out of him. He stares ahead.

Oh, Woman!

He pauses.

Lips faintly reddened, white makeup spread cool and milky on your nape. Oh, woman, do not press those rubbery breasts so hard against me. Do not titillate my back so slyly with your delicate fish-like fingertips. Oh, woman, do not caress my face with your fragrant sighs. Yes, woman, stop playing the flirt! Oh, woman—how wretched to be woman.

"I suggest it's particularly wretched to be a woman if she's exploited. You tell us you stole from the mother, and the love affair with your married friend is illicit."

I no sooner say this than I want to bite my tongue. I had said too much, too soon. Peel the onion. Layer by layer. Time is up.

Taking his fez and wedging it back on his head, Sakutarô brandishes his cane and leaves with a hint of bravura.

I feel wonderfully lucky to have spent the last thirty years with Sigmund Freud, Melanie Klein and Wilfred Bion. Lucky for Sakutarô, too, if it turns out he not only talks the talk, but walks the walk.

"So, esteemed partner," I muse. "You want to understand the natural workings of your mind. Your first statement zaps us with thoughts of suicide. Before we can catch our breath you say a woman shreds your heart so you'll keep away from all women. We'll call that your monastic solution. But what if just maybe, you're one of those rare human beings who takes on the devil—Sigmund and Melanie and Wilfred, for example—or Jacob his dark angel?"

NOTES FROM ABOVEGROUND

Drifted over my sweaty cuff

Cuffs indicate a Western shirt and a jacket—except for bureaucrats and businessmen, unusual apparel in provincial Maebashi. Sakutarô adored strutting around town wearing his self-designed suits, spats, a cane, and sometimes even a red-tasseled Turkish fez.

And gaped spellbound at passing trams

Maebashi's pitiful little trolley ran down a street only slightly wider than an alleyway—no comparison with the streetcars running up and down the capital's grand, tree-lined boulevards. He longed always to be in Tokyo or anywhere but in Maebashi.

I roamed the banks of the Toné yesterday

One of the writer's favorite haunts. In those days the Toné formed the western boundary of Maebashi. The river's usually lethargic current becomes swift only during the vernal thaw or the typhoon season.

To be truthful, whatever I do tears are my life

Historically, the Japanese have a special affinity for tears. From a Western viewpoint, tears invite distasteful hyperbole —in Japan, one needs a bucketful to wet the mats or, in the cliché idiom, one's kimono sleeve. Sakutarô implies a longing for Nakako (later baptismal name, Elena). Nakako and he were madly in love. Alas, he was a college dropout with neither a job nor hope for the future—not husband material. So Nakako's parents arranged in September 1909 for her to marry Dr. Satô, a Christian and a gynecologist. He ran a lying-in hospital a ten or fifteen-minute train ride from Maebashi. Meanwhile, the unemployed Sakutarô continued to live at home supported by his wealthy physician father who fiercely objected to his dissolute lifestyle and involvement in free verse.

I no longer spend my days yearning for her

He refers to Nakako, by this time married four years.

Last night I stole some money

The five-yen note Sakutarô took could rent a modest two-room house for a month.

"Haven't we passed Yamashina yet?" she asks

Yamashina refers to a famous scene in a popular 1900 novel. A mother engineers a divorce between her son and his beloved. The son's wife developed TB and thus cannot produce a healthy heir. The couple's final glimpse of each other is at Yamashina Station, where their trains pass each other. Elena in those days was an ambulatory patient in a TB sanitarium. Critics consider this work, titled "Night Train," Sakutarô's earliest masterpiece.

Snuggling together in grief

In 1913, not even a properly married couple would dare "snuggle together" on a public conveyance. This would be viewed as lewd conduct. Sakutarô speaks metaphorically.

Keep away from women

These words display Sakutarô's flippantly ironic side. Every statement derives from what he considered the Christian "take" on male attitudes toward women, and is thus opposite his meaning. He couldn't grasp why God first programs males to conquer women, but proscribes sex outside of marriage. However, Sakutarô regarded God's plan a huge success—it makes every man feel miserably guilty!

NOTES FROM UNDERGROUND

Sakutarô arrives on time. Plainly dressed. No snazzy suit. No spats. No fez. No cane. Walking in with his head down, he goes straight to the couch.

Crowds had gathered under the blossoms. Wondering how they might be amusing themselves, I figured that I, too, would stand under the cherry trees. But something chilled me, and I did nothing but shed tears over already scattered petals. I wept merely out of self-pity, not because at high noon on this spring day I'd witnessed anything sad.

"I have a theory," I say, somewhat brightly. "Theories, of course, are a dime a dozen. Whatever theories occur as we work, I'll have no problem sharing. You remain the sole authority. If my suppositions make no sense, that's the end of it. I suggest you're differentiating the external world from the internal. In the middle of happy crowds and lovely cherry blossoms at high noon, inwardly you experience chilly weather."

It's not the intimidating dreams of a suckling that night after night quake my soul.

"Freud thought that negatives don't exist in—what he called—the unconscious. For the moment, let us assume Freud is right. You claim it's not the intimidating dreams of a suckling that quake your soul. Let's turn that negative into a positive. What does intimidate the dreaming suckling?"

No response.

Then it hits me. "Wouldn't the most intimidating dream for a suckling be to find itself alone, abandoned, without a feeding and comforting breast? That would quake a suckling's soul. Yes, indeed."

Closing his eyes, Sakutarô's taut face reflects a plunge into a deep reverie. When he speaks, his words float from a great distance.

You seem to be gazing at the blue surface of the evening sea where fireflies flit. I sidle up to you as you sit there relaxed, staring into the distance. Swells gently lap the shore, then recede. Is it because of the way the moon brightens tonight that a string of jellyfish seems to quiver far down the strand? Sitting speechless, we face each other...

He breaks off speaking.

I respond, "Like a string of jellyfish under a bright moon, so fantasies, like dreams, can also quiver in the mind."

Exploding, he barks,

Because I remain persistently an unrestrained fish-in-heat, now of all times my hand reaches out to restrain what had firmly swelled.

Sakutarô's chest heaves. Danger crackles. Abruptly relaxing, he speaks quietly.

Accustomed now to life in a bottomless well, my sightless fish feels pleased with his timeless, gloomy home. Not a ripple on his icy blue. Today as always, time drips like fig milk.

"Drips like fig milk. Can you elaborate?"

The scales of this wriggling fish glow even in fathomless water. How lonely where pale textures groan. Presupposing that he has always fled the world of inspiration, existing alone...dim...chilled...never sighing even once like a living creature—then his thirst will be incomprehensible.

With a flat tone, casually he says,

Whenever I despair of life and happen to glance into the well's unplumbed depths, I find the fins of my sightless fish teeming with élan. His wonderfully pale ecstasy then instantly becomes my private joy.

"I'm going to trot out yet another theory. I suggest you're talking about self-pleasure." Silence. Continued silence. Ten minutes worth. All the while he keeps blinking his eyes. Otherwise, he doesn't move a muscle. I keep hearing in my head, "Time drips like fig milk." Then my thoughts become as insubstantial as jellyfish in moonlight.
He sighs.

I plunge this deeply into disquiet because nobody mothers me.

It is my turn to jerk my head as though receiving a blow. "Yes," I say. "Abandoned. Despairing of life. Nobody to mother you, no breast to provide and protect and comfort. You turn to the penis, your unrestrained fish-in-heat, dripping semen and providing instant joy. For all that, self-pleasure leaves you existing alone, dim, chilled, suffering from Incomprehensible Thirsts."

I'm not a bad person at heart, but because my eyes are so blameless, reading the words of Jesus bewildered me. Thus did my Guide dupe me and dump me into this brimstone Hell. Even my daily prayers are empty now, and there's no one but myself to hold me tight. Whoever might indulge myself but me?

"The problem with holding yourself tight is it's not working. You are not comforted by self-indulgence, by what you call private joy. Nor does Jesus help. On the contrary, Jesus bewilders you. Prayers fail. Neither self-pleasure nor religious faith rescue you from a sense of abandonment, experienced like a brimstone hell."

I sink so into disquiet simply because I have no one to mother me. Ah, light—brighten my path to Hell!

"Freud described Hell as the Unpleasure Principle. Someone irreplaceable relieves the agonies of unpleasure. Humans are cradled in a life endlessly rocking, needing to be fed, cleaned, caressed, held, comforted, assured. By another! Not the self, praying or masturbating. That way lies damnation. A sexual knot alone ties us to this world." I want to say more, but this time I successfully bite my tongue, reminding myself this is only our second session. Peel the onion.

Thus, I don't bring up that second-floor steakhouse where perversely he had turned away from The Breast to gape at passing trams. Sakutarô seems exhausted and with effort lifts himself off the couch and leaves. Even a genius writer can't suck life from his thumb. I sit a long time in my chair behind the couch, deep in thought.

Why is Sakutarô here? What is the mystery he wants to solve? What is he trying to unravel? discover? cure? Suddenly, I glimpse what Sakutarô means by his having spent a lifetime trying to understand himself. Why is he his own worst enemy? He ends up starving in a steakhouse, for heaven's sake. What kind of sense does that make?

On a glorious spring day, in the midst of happy crowds and bursting cherry blossoms, he's bawling and feeling chilled no less. Mother's a goddess, and he steals from her. Sakutarô's madly in love and drives his love away. He strolls along a favorite river and is preoccupied with suicide. For salvation, Sakutarô turns to self-pleasure. What gives? I tingle with anticipatory joy. Just maybe Sakutarô and I will attain a better understanding of "the natural workings of mind." His mind. My mind. All of our minds.

Will Sakutarô throw light on what Freud termed *The Death Instinct*, inborn destructive powers that threaten human well being? Is it true, "In sin did my mother conceive me"? Sakutarô's ability to hear a suckling crying out in terror for its mother in some internal region of his mind and to recognize he is that suckling doomed to live life in a brimstone hell without her, leaves me breathless. That way salvation lies.

Meanwhile, Sakutarô struggles with incomprehensible thirsts. Little wonder suicide jumped out early in our work.

NOTES FROM ABOVEGROUND

Crowds had gathered under the blossoms

The joys of viewing cherry blossoms parallel the joys our ancestors felt when they danced around the Maypole. No such joy for Sakutarô. As his heart weeps over its isolation, the ephemerality of the blossoms further chills him.

My sightless fish feels pleased

This fish is sightless because a penis, though it has a head, lacks eyes.

Time drips like fig milk

It's impossible to read any reference to fish in Sakutarô's verse without considering the phallic import. Fig milk possibly refers to semen. Because in antiquity peoples throughout the Mediterranean perceived the fruit as the vulva and the leaves as the phallus, eating figs understandably came to symbolize erotic ecstasy. The fruit became associated with fecundity and breasts. Artemis, the universal mother and nurturer of the young, changed herself into a fig tree styled "the tree of many breasts."

Because I have no one to mother me

Sakutarô's mother in fact indulged him, consistently providing him money for booze, books and travel.

NOTES FROM UNDERGROUND

Arriving a few minutes late, Sakutarô wears a tweed jacket with a knotted green scarf around his neck. On the dashing side, his entrance jaunty, he bounces onto the couch.

Throwing a hand in the air, he pronounces,

At daybreak on this early May outing, our Shade Tree Club will scatter silver glitter over the streets. Each club member fondles the nape of a young girl—feeling as light-headed as if he'd been smoking a cigar.

He inhales on an imaginary cigar, loudly exhaling through pursed lips.

The basis of the spectrum is red. The pit of the litchi nut is red. The consummate human being is a virgin.

And summarizing with a flourish,

Young girls epitomize the essence of the soul!

"Hmmm," I respond dryly.
Visibly sagging, Sakutarô unties the green scarf.

Whenever sun sets in Tokyo, I become an anemic fish-in-heat. Day after day, I suffer the agonies of this curse. By now, I'm gasping for air.

I say, "It's good you loosened your scarf."
Sakutarô roars back,

Oh, Lord, holy God of lust. I spade the ground, plow the soil, and day after day groom Thy herd. May has come now to the fields, to the hills. Let there be glory, glory, glory to the Lord of lust and to His train! Amen.

"Theologian Freud observed a few things about your God of lust. Glory! Glory! Sex! Sex!"
Frowning, knocked off balance for an instant, he pushes on,

Verily, God's will fills my heart and His will is my will. But I won't be in the least upset if my creed differs from God's commands, for I am my own god.

Sakutarô again waves a "cigar" imperiously.

Well, then, Jehovah my friend, great egotistical God, let's exchange cups of friendship and salute the Son of Man.

"That must be you," I say. Sudden silence. Gone the cigar.

Instead, he touches a hand gingerly to his cheek.

This day: bitter anguish. After having my rotted tooth painfully pulled.

I want to shout for joy. For his sake. Sakutarô's not mad. "You may be your own god, but meanwhile, you recognize your need for a dentist." He doesn't laugh. I find his sanity wonderful, though glad for the couch, as Sakutarô can't see me grinning from ear to ear.

Gathering himself, he says quietly,

I grieve for my superfluous hands because by nature I'm sensitive to the extreme. My hands flutter constantly overhead or dangle in lonely radiance about my chest. Transformed into steel, my hands despondently burrow into the soil. My pitiful, sensitive hands burrow into the soil.

I suggest his craft, that of a writer, makes him despondent in that he doesn't do ordinary physical labor, such as farming. Sakutarô's an artist. In a certain sense, his hands are superfluous. At the same time, he likens them to steel; they have the strength to create powerful structures with words. His self-pleasuring, however, makes it difficult for him to appreciate their artistic powers.

Fish steadily swim downstream, quickening this shallow brook. Oh, Elena, however far from you I may be, I'll visit you on my pilgrimage. The rockfish lingers in my grip as I yearn tenderly for you.

"You yearn for a sexual relationship with her."
To my surprise, Sakutarô laughs with abandon.

Every day I shed tears trying to believe the unbelievable.

"Such as?" I ask.

Whatever stems from selfless love is more perilous than poisonous plants. My brothers have fasted—just for me!

He flings his hands dismissively.

Oh, God, if that is absolutely true, then I intend to cross myself before I'm crucified and openly confess my every dark deed.

I jump in, "Your brothers in Christ, fasting just for you. Ha! Don't believe it, you say. Supposed selfless love is more perilous than poisonous plants. Why? It's a lie. I suggest your theology very much parallels that of Freud. Both you and Freud observe that sex is fundamental to life. Front and center. And sex is forever claimant, ruthless and violent. How'd you put it?

"Human ontology is defined by sexual status. Your brothers-in-Christ turn this fact around. They crucify sex, insisting love will prevail. In your experience, that's not how it works. Believing that requires you to falsify the facts. Freud stated this famously, namely, ego is first and foremost a 'body ego.' The body is where it all happens, whether a toothache or an erection. The body flaunts the nape of a young girl. Virginal genitals epitomize the essence of the soul. Confessing sexual misdeeds in no way lessens the primacy of the body. Confession solves nothing."

Sakutarô leaves in high spirits. I feel the same way. His rotted tooth is a gift from the tooth fairy! She brought him the incomparable gift of sanity and hands of measureless artistic power.

NOTES FROM ABOVEGROUND

Each club member fondles the nape of a young girl

Caressing a woman in public could result in a citation. Even now, Japanese determinedly avoid physical displays, particularly in public. The nape is the most erotic focus of a kimono-clad woman.

The pit of the litchi nut is red
the consummate human being is a virgin

The redder the litchi nut, the fresher and tastier the fruit. Between age forty-three when his wife left him and age fifty-two when he remarried, Sakutarô told friends who urged him to find a mate that he had but one criterion—she must be a virgin. He used the English word. We assume his second wife met that standard.

Oh, Lord, holy God of lust

This marvel of sarcasm is another tongue-in-cheek slash at Christian sexual ethics. God is lustful. Why can't he let us be lustful, too? Sakutarô felt plagued into his forties by Christian teachings on sex learned from the Bible and Victorian missionaries.

Oh, Elena, however far from you I may be

He wrote these words three months after the love of his life, Nakako, received her baptismal name, Elena (Helen). Conversion removed her further from the possibility of his ever possessing her.

My brothers have fasted just for me

This no doubt refers to members of Sakutarô's Sunday Bible class, which he attended into his thirties. At that time, men and women usually attended separate classes. The brothers, his classmates, may have been asked to pray or fast for his spiritual welfare.

NOTES FROM UNDERGROUND

Sakutarô's appearance startles me. From riches back to rags, he hasn't bothered to shave, clothes and body evidencing abandonment.

Shuffling to the couch, lying down and sounding forced, Sakutarô says,

Look—my dice in the air. There's a row of tables. The eyes of my fellow players aflame with love. Look—the ace of hearts turned up on the green gaming table.

Sakutarô barks out irritably,

Prayed over Elena, as well!

"You gambled for love and lost? Is that what you're saying?"

My body, my body, who would enfeeble this body?

He crosses himself.

Secretly I kiss the Cross. Lord, have mercy on me! Mine the path of a heretical faith, my companions the vipers of lust. I cling nevertheless to the Lord, the true Lord of the Holy Catholic Church!

Crossing himself again, he adds,

Actually, I'm alien to prayer. How dare lips enflamed by rotgut defile the name of the Lord? My songs are poems from Hell. Lips that praise demonic love—how dare they sing a sacred hymn?

"The problem, I suggest, is not that you're alien to prayer. Quite the opposite. You speak a great deal of religion. Secretly you kiss the Cross. It's a major focus of your mind. The question is why you keep secret your involvement and preoccupation with religious life. Religion is a major activity of the human mind.

"No culture is known which existed without religion. Yet, as Wilfred Bion pointed out, religion is still peculiarly neglected in psychoanalysis, even though it's certainly as pervasive an activity as sex. If a human being were spoken of as having no alimentary canal, Bion said, that would be a monster indeed. In fact, it would bear no resemblance to the human animal. The same is true if one ignores the religious life of a person."

I cannot endure the secret pangs of my iniquities. Santa Maria. Santa Maria. Holy Mother, have mercy on me. Amen.

"You can't reconcile life in the body—the secret pangs of your iniquities—with the sacred. And you certainly can't reconcile the Holy Mother with flaming lust and demonic love. Santa Maria!"

Again Sakutarô implores,

Holy Mother, have mercy upon me. Amen.

Long silence.

Heads up! There's a gold mine in the sky.

He shakes his head slowly, emphatically nay-saying.

Singing sadly, tears falling, I alone will dig the soil, dig the blue-tattooed earth.

"No pie-in-the-sky religion for you. Fool's gold. You're keeping your feet on the ground."

Again he makes the sign of the Cross.

Holy Mother, have mercy upon me.

Unbearable grief seeps slowly into Sakutarô.

My Love! Don't fear your contagion. Disease has always been a human being's grief.

"Always humans have to deal with disease, such as Elena's fatal illness, your rotten tooth. Our bodies are endlessly vulnerable to contagion."

I've no idea how to make a living.

Quietly he adds,

I haven't eaten yet today.

"Our bodies require endless maintenance. In sickness or in health, every day somehow we have to scrounge a living." Very deliberately Sakutarô swings his feet on to the floor, gets up and walks to the window. I swivel my chair in his direction and wait. Time passes. He stares intently out the window.

The fifth floor of an empty building, all nine windows permanently shut. The silence of thick curtains.

He puts a hand in front of his eyes. "I propose to use your actions these last few minutes as though they had occurred in a dream—your getting off the couch, looking out the window, your puzzling statements about that empty building across the street with its nine windows permanently shut, the silence of thick curtains, and your ending the dramatization by putting a hand in front of your eyes, blocking off the view.

"With Freud I assume you're telling us something the same as you do in a dream. What that is only you know. It's your communication. At any rate, I have a conjecture about your pantomime dream. If it doesn't ring a bell for you, there's an end to my theory. Here's my conjecture. The fifth floor of that empty building refers to the five senses. You put your hand in front of your eyes. When you do that, you can't use your eyes to register the real world."

Sakutarô paces the room.

The sleuth nevertheless paces from one corner of the room to the other. A wooden chair in the center of the room has a hidden electric device that's lethal.

Moving my desk chair to the middle of the room, he pretends to trip over it.

I say, "Ah, now I too can see there's a wooden chair in the center of the room which has a hidden electric device that's lethal."

What a pity that this ill-fated investigator is so oblivious of that chair.

"He's blind. A pity."

The sleuth will be absolutely unaware of what's on the wall behind him—the painted corpse of the poisoned child. The pasty obstinacy of death, unpleasant feelings in that remote realm of mystic wonder. This solitary individual trembles, peering intently into his thoughts. Oh, my miserable, my sickly sleuth.

"Yes. Alone, a solitary individual, you're unaware of what's happening. Here, however, there are two of us. We both can see your pantomime; whereas the sightless sleuth remains absolutely unaware. Without your five senses—and mine, our common sense—you find yourself in a remote realm of mystic wonder. Without common sense, your life has the pasty obstinacy of death. Now, what might you be talking about with that wooden chair that has a hidden but lethal electric device? My guess, it's a reference to self-pleasuring. Ejaculating through self-pleasure is lethal to sex."

My interest in sex wretchedly wanes. My hands resolutely joined in prayer, my eyes sightless.

"Hands in prayer or hands in self-pleasure—either way you destroy sexual life. Both make sex wretched."

Sakutarô bursts out,

Go ahead and die!

pointing a finger at a corner of the room.

The glowing tips of fingers waxy in death will send your soul reeling into the sky. Then surely you'll be able to see Omega's chalky eye—your true personality.

Sakutarô scratches his head, a quizzical expression on his face. Wrinkling his brow, he says, eyeing me,

Humans seem catlike.

"Make up your mind. You can't have it both ways. You claim your true personality is that of omega. Then you say, I'm not omega. I'm catlike."

Look! The kiss of love vivid on my glove. Yes, since green by now grows green, my soul sprouts buds and senses itself aglow. Facing a foe fabricated from the soil, my flesh quivers in rapturous glee, and the eyes of sensitivity open vividly onto space.

"Fling open the five senses," I say. "Throw back those thick, silencing curtains. Open vividly the eyes of sensitivity. Let flesh quiver in rapturous glee."

Ah, on days when my flesh makes me swim pathetically in searing heat, I torment and abuse women.

"That's the trouble with sex. You play the ace of hearts and you may or may not win your gamble. Suppose your woman gets desperately ill. Meanwhile sexual heat is searing. Agony! The pain makes you want to torment and abuse women."

Sakutarô sits down in my desk chair, still in the middle of the room. He rocks back and forth, watching the clock. When our time is up, he rises and saunters out.

It never ceases to amaze me how difficult this work is. Sakutarô already looks exhausted and beat up. Why? It sounds so simple: "Say what's on your mind." There is no other rule—besides not breaking the furniture. What could be easier, perched comfortably on a couch in an air conditioned room, enjoying complete privacy and a listener's full attention? Until you try it!

NOTES FROM ABOVEGROUND

Prayed over Elena, as well

After her baptism, Elena made concerted efforts to discourage Sakutarô's attention. Soon she refused to answer his letters. Once she even sent him a blank piece of paper; that incident infuriated and incapacitated him for days.

I alone will dig the soil

Digging implies a shovel, a phallic image. Earth is female.

My Love! Don't fear your contagion

Sakutarô refers, of course, to Elena who suffered from tuberculosis.

The sleuth nevertheless paces
from one corner of the room to the other

Detectives are decisive men who solve problems logically, a type Sakutarô admires.

A wooden chair in the center of the room
has a hidden electric device that's lethal

This image suggests the possible hazards of assuming authority, which a chair may symbolize. Inability to see the lethal aspects of the chair brings to mind the blindness of the psyche and the hazards of examining one's self.

Facing a foe fabricated from the soil

Sakutarô refers to the Old Testament story of God shaping Adam-Man from the soil.

NOTES FROM UNDERGROUND

Sakutarô is late. When he arrives he avoids eye contact and slides almost furtively onto the couch. He begins a chant-like recitation.

The path I walk intent on remembering the dead. The path I take to offer chrysanthemums. The path that makes my body drip with blood. The path of cabbage, of meat, and fish. The path of lust.

It suddenly occurs to me. "You put your hand in front of your eyes at our last session. I suggest your chant gets in the way of talking with me."

A wistful tug skews a corner of his mouth. He takes a deep breath and snaps himself into a no-nonsense mental state.

I'm terribly sorry I bruised your lips when I kissed you yesterday. After returning home, I stored my fish in an amber rock and later let it swim through that miniature landscape in the tray.

"What's the kissing about?"
He responds quietly,

Skylark cuisine. Devotedly holding the dish of cooked skylark, I'll walk meekly to your left.

"Consider a theory. Perhaps you're talking about cunnilingus. So violently you kiss her labia, you bruise them. Since your fish got into the act swimmingly, my conjecture is you're describing a fantasy during self-pleasuring."
He speaks carefully,

Reverently carrying a dish of cooked skylark, a young girl walks through this somewhat chilly, rime-frosted morning. I was leaning then against a tree along the avenue and peering intently at the gaps between her slender, milky cream-coated fingers. I hanker to steal that tasty skylark dish and eat it.

"And so you do. In fantasy."
He replies, a lilt in his voice,

Creak light-heartedly, four-wheeled coach. Creak past blue-windowed buildings and through the azure skies of sparkling fish and birds. Creak light-heartedly, four-wheeled coach.

"What is deeper in the heart of things than a woman's genitals?"

Sakutarô snarls, taking me aback.

Distinctions forever agonize. Oh, eyes that would take in everything.

I jump in. "When you look directly at a woman's genitals, they evoke agony. What is more distinctive than the differences between the sexes—between male and female?"

You who came into existence like a headless baby girl born from beyond the grave, oh, eyes! Look intently into the skies, into the abyss of unbearable agonies. Oh, eyes! Waken from your sleep.

"You want to open your eyes to the facts of life. Except, when you do, seeing evokes unbearable agony."

Something lurking out there emerged from behind a distant willow and gradually approached. But look! It held a silver weapon frozen in its hands, frozen in the darkness. That something quite clearly wielded a weapon—holding it high above his brow.

"You're suffering what Freud described as castration anxiety. You see a woman's genitals and if hers are so mutilated then no reason the same won't happen to yours. The difference between the sexes fosters violence, something wielding a weapon held high above its brow."

Sakutarô sits forward, his legs remaining on the couch.

Uncommonly uncanny hands appear from the abyss of the ground into which I stare. Legs appear. A protruding head appears.

He pauses,

Say, my friends,

continuing but sounding bewildered,

whatever sort of geese are these?

"I'll share a secret—babies. Those are babies: b-a-b-i-e-s!"

From the abyss of the ground into which I stare, a moronic look on my face, hands appear, legs appear. An intrusively protruding head appears.

Sakutarô breaks off.

Death.

"No. Birth. Babies. Talk about distinctions and differences now! The woman's genitals are delicious as a cooked skylark. But, they're also the ground of being, the uncanny abyss from which you and each of us emerge. Can you have babies? No. All you have—at least so far—is your penis. Is that comparable to the power of a woman giving birth?"
He lies back down, trying to speak with calm.

Haruna, let your summit glow. Sparkle over the Toné, Haruna, glow as though you're at prayer!

Sakutarô's agitation returns.

All around me green bamboo glistens to a point. I dash naked into the bamboo thicket that grows with such great verve. Then, kneeling on the dark red soil and maniacally

**gnashing my teeth, I frantically pray. I look through gaps
in the bamboo grass at glittering high-noon skies. With
determined finality, I file my fingers to a point.**

"Earlier," I say, "you look through the gaps between the
young girl's slender, milky cream-coated fingers, at her genitals. Then geese start popping out. They completely
unnerve you. You dash naked into the bamboo thicket. You
fall on the dark red soil of the woman's vagina, in the bamboo thicket of her pubic hair, realizing her genitals link to
the uncanny powers that create life. Looking through gaps
in the bamboo grass—gaps like the vulva—you maniacally
gnash your teeth. Why? Bamboo like geese grow with such
great verve. You gnash your teeth at the fecundity of sex."

Sakutarô replies instantly,

**Nail my hands. Nail my feet. Attach me to a cross. Scourge
my lasciviousness. In agony I gnash my teeth. The skies
roar. Earth roars. Pale blood streams down my limbs, dripping furiously. Bolts of lightning rip from the sky to rend
and shred my flesh. Unashamed now of my nakedness, I
gnash my teeth on the cross and pray.**

"In the world of sexual life, you're no big deal. That you
will not tolerate. So you create not babies but a giant fantasy, a moral universe. Agonies and lightnings and shreddings
of flesh and crucifixions and scourgings and dripping
blood—these will take your mind off sex."

He rises from the couch; before I blink, he is gone. I sit
until time for the session ends—some fifteen minutes.
Where's Sakutarô's pain? What grief propels him so abruptly from the session? I'm guessing it's recognizing he's no big
deal. Even a genius writer must submit to the accursed
fecundity of biologic life.

I recall Bion once saying that in every consulting room there ought to be two rather frightened people. If not, one wonders why they are bothering to find out what everyone knows. Of course, without Freud and Oedipus what sense could I have made of his astonishing associations? I find it comforting that the Japanese Sakutarô, ten thousand miles from Vienna, speaks like someone on Freud's couch one hundred years ago at 19 Berggasse. As Sakutarô and I are learning, it's when one tries it that one discovers two rather frightened people.

Notes from Aboveground

These works appeared in the wake of increasing tensions with Elena, whom he was still pursuing five years after her marriage. Sakutarô had just turned twenty-eight.

The path of cabbage, of meat

Both imply Western-style cuisine. Cabbage is known for producing flatulence. He confesses interest in what's alien.

I'm terribly sorry I bruised your lips when I kissed you yesterday

The vast majority of Japanese in 1914 had only read about passionate kissing. After "flicks" were introduced from the West, government censors consistently excised kissing scenes. If Elena is the one he's kissing, she would resist, so bruises are a possibility.

Legs appear, a protruding head appears

Mother Earth involved in a breech birth? The hand-head-feet order rudely surprises.

Haruna, let your summit glow ...glow as though you're at prayer!

Perhaps a writer can create verse exuding a glow similar to Haruna's by linking it to radiation capable of attacking the cancer of psychic affliction. Sakutarô's work did impact modern Japanese verse like a surge of radiation.

NOTES FROM UNDERGROUND

Again Sakutarô arrives late, looking the worse for wear, but this time he walks directly to the couch and begins resolutely.

My hands have been electrified. My hands are platinum.

"Hands of a writer."

My hands ache with rheumatic pain. My hands glow in heartwood. My hands glow on fish.

"Hands of self-pleasure."
Without batting an eye he continues his litany.

Hands glow on gravestones. Hands glow brightly.

Wherever I go, my hands have already detached from their arms.

"Again you're talking about castration anxiety, linking it to the effeminate nature of your craft. It's not your penis which is cut off but your hands. You downplay Byron and Heine. Are your hands, powerful masculine tools, only to be used to scribble romantic stuff, causing them to ache with rheumatic pains like an old woman's? or merely to glow from pleasuring your fish-in-heat?"

He raises both hands in front of his face, turning them back and around.

My hands glow in space where their fingers disclose revelations. My gleaming metallic wrists, pointedly polished, blind me, rend my flesh, and chip my bones.

"At our first conversation you claim your writings reveal the natural workings of your mind. Your fingers disclose revelations. As Freud observed, that's a herculean feat, a difficult and dangerous business."

Horrors! Horrors! Pale radium sickens my hands and agonizes my fingers.

"The problem is you don't have normal hands. Your hands glow in some strange space from which your fingers disclose revelations. These disclosures blind you, rend your flesh and chip your bones. Your writings create horrors. Your work comes from deep within, as does radioactivity—and like radium, sickens your hands and agonizes your fingers."

He lies quiet, seeming relaxed.

I strum my guitar. I strum my guitar. Alone, I think back

on those days when twilight padded silently over the city's stonework, when trains ran overhead and various streetcars similarly passed me in silence as ceaseless as my love's never-ending stroll.

"You strum quietly, working your imagination, singing never-endingly of love."

Ah, life's solitudes! Arising from myself, these solitudes prowl about scattering seeds over the sidewalk: one of them sows, one waters, another and his progeny wear gleaming chapeaux—as twilight steals in. I sense how unimaginably removed I am from Tokyo, too far off for eyes to reach. I strum my guitar. I strum my guitar.

"You're an artist. Not because you're wearing a chapeau or a Turkish fez, but because you produce an active and living psychology arising from yourself. This is your work."

Sakutarô begins to cry.

An evening of unbearable griefs. Gently embracing my guitar, I gazed at Maebashi's single-story houses.

"Rather than losing yourself in a great metropolis, you stay in the town of your birth. You gaze at that single story, the story of your own person, embracing your destiny as a writer even though it gives rise to unbearable anguish. Contrast the gentle embracing of a guitar with the wild cacophony of a great city.

He wipes a tear with the back of his hand and lies perfectly still. Without warning, as at our last session, Sakutarô gets up and walks out.

I feel wonderfully moved, deep affection flowing through me. Where's the pain now? For his little town and its little lives, especially his own, that he holds in his hands; those hands disclose agonizing revelations.

Notes from Aboveground

My hands are platinum

Platinum relates to silver, which symbolizes Venus and lechery. Few images are as complex and variegated as the hand. Among many possibilities, the hand can serve as a figure of the self or its will, stand for the inner state of mind, symbolize a commitment to tell the truth, or through palm reading reveal one's character or fate. Sakutarô also associated hands with his ancestors' arthritic hands and with masturbation.

I strum my guitar

Sakutarô began studying the guitar when he was going on twenty-six, two years before he wrote "Guitarist". By then he'd flopped out of two colleges. His father, Dr. Hagiwara, still wanted him to get a degree, however, so he enrolled his son in prep courses at a private college in Tokyo. Feeling his individuality compromised, Sakutarô professed the classes to be an utter bore. He invested his energies in enjoying Tokyo's theater scene and richly exciting night life and soon dropped out.

I sense how unimaginably removed I am from Tokyo

In Maebashi, Sakutarô longs for the capital, especially its anonymity. In Tokyo he could wear fancy hats or a Turkish fez and not be made an object of derision. Sakutarô experienced a meltdown when he met demands to conform. Constantly neutering cultural requirements and literary traditions, he questioned every constriction on his freedom. He perceived the life of his psyche, not his culture, as the basic ingredient of his aesthetic. In a word, he saw himself as a work of art demanding expression. Little else mattered.

I gazed at Maebashi's single-story houses

These humble houses emphasize Sakutarô's bitter grief over not being in Tokyo, where one finds countless tall structures, spacious houses and sprawling apartment buildings.

Session
Bill Collector

NOTES FROM UNDERGROUND

My conversational partner is late. I spend the time mulling about him. He never does show. I doubt he heard I expect him to pay for missed sessions, so now we'll get to thrash out that problem.

NOTES FROM UNDERGROUND

A new month and the bill due. Sakutarô comes in looking quite friendly, dutifully going straight to the couch. He brings up payment first thing, apologizing for missing the previous session, the last one of the month. "It's your session," I say. "How you use the time is up to you."

Sakutarô becomes somewhat angry. Suppose illness or family problems prevent his coming? What's he supposed to do about that! I say, "I appreciate that. Life is endlessly beset by the unexpected."

He gets off the couch and says he will sit up hereafter.

"I have no problem with that," I shrug. "The only rule is that you can't break the furniture. You can sit in a corner, if you like. Or stand. Or stand on your hands. Whichever nook and posture suits." He unleashes a string of what I presume are Japanese expletives. I reply "I'm helpless without my translator, but two and two are still four in all languages. Arithmetic is universal."

He states my intransigence is making him lose it, and he doesn't mean the money.

"If my safety is at risk, then we have two options. If you want to continue our conversations, with your permission and my authority as a physician, we can put you in hospital. We can then talk safely by using physical restraints. Or we interrupt the work until it can be continued safely in the office."

He says he finds me utterly unfair.

"Certainly our relationship is unequal," I say. "For example, I expect you to arrange your vacations to dovetail with mine. And I expect you to pay for missed sessions, regardless of circumstances." He snorts he has no idea what he is supposed to gain from so much rigmarole. "It's obvious what I get from our work, namely my fee. What you get from the conversations is not my business. Since you're present, you can decide what if anything you get from this work."

Sakutarô stands up and walks to the door. Stopping, he reaches in his pocket and pulls out a piece of paper and walking back to the couch throws a dirty, partially torn, and crumpled check on it as he leaves. I uncrumple the check. It is for all the sessions.

Nothing matters more in my relationship with Sakutarô than keeping time and money straight. When he comes across with the correct arithmetical quantity, as here, there is rejoicing in heaven. The only motivation for this difficult work is a love of truth. The most vivid truth, without doubt, is that each of us is ruthlessly and forever subject to the constraints of time and money, no quarter ever given. Sakutarô, for all his preciousness and grandness, throws down the check as he throws himself on the couch. The sum computes.

Any sinner with respect for arithmetic has a chance to enter the kingdom, and heaven rejoices.

NOTES FROM ABOVEGROUND

To show Sakutarô paying his bill by check is an obvious fiction that dovetails with the conceit he is on the couch of a 21st century Los Angeles psychoanalyst. No Japanese of Sakutarô's milieu would pay any bill by personal check.

After subscribing to the 1931 Geneva Checks Act, Japan passed domestic legislation to order and standardize check writing. The primary users, however, were big corporations and not individuals. Even in the 21st century, the average private citizen in Japan rarely pays a bill by check. It would, indeed, be extremely difficult for almost any Japanese, whether living in a cosmopolitan area or not, to discover an acquaintance—other than a foreigner—with a private checking account.

The Japanese custom is to pay cash for services rendered as well as for retail purchases. Certain cash payments have long demanded special formalities. Japan's ruling classes have been inhibited by a centuries long, Confucian oriented aversion to handling cash, charging interest, or "gouging" others to make profits, activities considered "dirty."

In fact, there are stories of samurai fathers refusing to teach their sons basic mathematical skills because they associated arithmetic with the acquisition of money and the activities of merchants, a despised class. This was, of course, far more the rule in Sakutarô's day than it is now among the younger generation. The transfer of cash as payment for services, as opposed to goods bought at a store, consequently required certain rituals. The money was inserted in an envelope, and at times wrapped in paper, before being transferred.

Even today, Japanese businessmen tip the concierge in this manner. In no imaginable Japanese context, past or present, would a patient ever even think of crumpling his payment and tossing it haphazardly onto a couch. This shocking and abhorrent insult would motivate any physician, dentist, psychiatrist, lawyer or teacher to refuse association with such a brazenly barbaric and wickedly unappreciative individual.

Nowadays Japanese accept credit cards.

NOTES FROM UNDERGROUND

Sakutarô arrives on time. He looks directly at me when I open the door, nods and walks briskly to the couch. Unmistakably, this man has both feet on the ground. When money's kept straight, this happens routinely in psychoanalytic work.

He says,

A crude thieving cur howls at the moon. Why am I forever behaving like this? Oh, cur—pasty, ill-starred cur.

I interject. "You refer to yourself as a thieving cur, and yet you paid your bill in full last session."

He takes a deep breath. My observation enables him to access a different region of his mind.

There's a hole in that dark green wall of the bar I'm in

tonight—a hole behind that framed picture of the sorrowing Madonna. I put my eye to the opening and peer through it. For some strange reason nobody knows a thing about that grotesque and distant realm beyond the hole. Even when I'm drunk, my blanched ghost of a saké cup tells me nothing of those...

He pauses.

...*unknowns!*

In a sing-song, he repeats quietly,

In the wall of the bar I'm in tonight, a hole.

"I suggest you are forever behaving out of curiosity. You investigate realms of the unknown, and that takes courage as well as making large demands on your time and money. Your writings, which you liken to an ill-starred cur howling at the moon, publish your findings to the world. What is puzzling is that your investigative work falls under such condemnation."

Weapons in either hand, a masked brigand struts arrogantly up the road. He peers intently at someone or at something beyond. Sad to say, however, this blackguard pays no attention to what's behind him—that endless, murky clapboard fence of his unknown crimes. He's a knave clad in silver garments that fluoresce in the dark. Grotesque as he may be, this is one one-eyed brigand no eye has ever seen.

"I'm reminded of Freud in Vienna. The gynecologists thought he was a peeping Tom. Freud investigated sexual life, like you, and was also thought a pasty, ill-starred cur."

Lord! Tell me that the sins I've obviously committed are obviously sins that I've committed.

He shakes his head, holding up and wagging a finger.

I'll confess to having novenas said for the holy idols of a heretical sect.

"I suggest you're referring to the heretical sect of scientists and artists who recognize sexual life as a distant realm marked by unknowns. These need to be identified and made understandable. Your devotion to looking at sex scientifically, what you liken to saying novenas, tarnishes you as an arrogant, one-eyed brigand, a knave, a howling cur."

Nevertheless, I believe in the Lord. I believe in the Lord. I truly believe in one Lord. Even if having been sick at the time stimulated my acts of penance, I leave everything to the Lord's will.

"Your talking with me, as well as your writings, make obvious that you are not leaving everything to the Lord. But why is your scientific and artistic activity a sin? Who says?"
As though from a great distance, he answers reflectively,

Behold, all sins have been recorded, yet I've not committed every one. Only shadowless phantoms of blue flame have actually been revealed to me, only ghosts of grief that vanish on the snow. Oh, how shall I cope with the bitter penance of those days? All are mere phantoms of blue flame. I watch blue flames blaze on every living thing.

"I suggest every living thing reveals a blue flame as insubstantial as a shadowless phantom or a ghost vanishing against a backdrop of bright and subliming snow. Such a flame cannot be recorded. Such a vanishing evanescence cannot be pinned down to enforce penance. It's gone in the twinkling of an eye."

Sakutarô sits up slowly and turns to me. I do not feel physically threatened but sense he is thinking through a thought. He speaks clinically.

Before the eagle *Awareness* flaps its wings, the songbird *Concept* invariably freezes to death.

He points to a corner of the room.

Notice the long cortege of *Time* approaching, the assembled black-robed priests chanting doleful dirges, heading for the hilltop shrine of *Poetry*.

He falls forward on his knees, pretending to hold with both arms a huge and invisible weight over his left shoulder. He staggers to his feet and collapses back on his knees, continuing to hold the great weight.

I lean toward him and ask, "What are you lugging that brings you to your knees? The weight of a mere songbird? Shadowless phantoms of blue flame? How is that possible?"

Huffing and puffing he answers,

The long cortege of *Time* carries the remains of *Frozen Concept*. This glorious cadaver will then be buried through our efforts and resurrected to eternal life.

"You suggest efforts to achieve eternal life kill the songbird and snuff the blue flame. Make permanent all sins by recording them, as do priests. Stuff works of art in the shrine of Poetry, as do artists. All they've done, you note ruefully, is resurrect cadavers for all eternity. These exist merely as frozen remains. Even if they exist forever, what is the point? One thing is obvious—lugging them around is crushing."

He gets off his knees and goes to the window. He presses his face against it and says, speaking rapidly,

Look! Here he comes: a silver wolf dashing at me from afar. Flourishing bolts of lightning from his fur and ardently sharpening his fangs, he dashes at me from the distance. Ah, the wolf's approach freezes me with horrifying dread. I'm somehow in awe of that beast's physical presence.

"'Look!' you're telling us. 'It's happening at this very instant. Here he comes.' Are you thinking of eternal life? Of course not. That awesome silver wolf dashing at you this very moment has your full attention."

He backs away from the window pane. A smile crosses his face. He sings out,

Green bamboo reaching up. Bamboo roots reaching through the soil, roots tapering to points, delicate fuzz reaching from the tips. Feebly misting fuzz reaches out, flickering faintly. Bamboo reaching from the frozen ground. Bamboo reaching sharply from the ground. Bamboo reaching up with unrelenting, all-out speed. Frozen joints awesome, bamboo reaching high into the blue. Bamboo—bamboo—bamboo—reaching up.

"You find the living world, animal and plant, awesome, whether flourishing bolts of lightning or reaching up with unrelenting, all-out speed."

He stands for a long time, staring out the window, then comes and sits back down on the couch. He looks away and says,

I wonder what I've accomplished over these many years. What have I learned? What have I observed?

He furrows his brow and turns to me.

All my secrets are sexual—what pallid mysteries!

"I suggest there's your answer. I know three people who would agree with you—Sigmund Freud, Melanie Klein and Wilfred Bion. They learned after years of talking and listening that human secrets are sexual. They dug the soil of Vienna and London and Los Angeles, you that of Maebashi and Tokyo. Same patterns. The experiences of the four of you turn up in variants and therefore invite scientific scrutiny of human sexual life."

He responds with a lilt to his voice,

Those secrets held voyeuristic glasses to my flesh. I personally thrashed myself. I whipped myself as though I were a packhorse. Then step by step, I set off on my pilgrimage.

He gets off the couch. At the door he turns around and says smiling,

Though this may be a grotesque tale, I was in fact unmarried at the time.

I don't know what to make of his final remark. Probably just having fun. Throughout the session Sakutarô's reference to the sorrowing Madonna and the hole behind her in the bar kept flitting through my mind. I feel bombarded by that venerable Church Father who insisted a woman is a beautiful temple built over a sewer. Peel the onion. Certainly one of the mysteries of sex is that it inspires horrifying dread.

Notes from Aboveground

A number of Sakutarô's writings published during 1914 and 1915 epitomize Rousseau's notion that human society corrupts the innocence of the naturally free man. Sakutarô wanted to believe he could exist in a "natural state," free from convention. Modernity in literature assumes such freedom impractical in a society weighed down by custom, ritual and reverence for the past.

Why am I forever behaving like this?
Oh, cur—pasty, ill-starred cur!

A favorite Sakutarô image is a dog howling at the moon. Born in the Year of the Dog, the writer howls at the cold moon—a realm only bards and animals can access, for they alone are uniquely at home in the dimension of primal fear and instinctive behavior.

Weapons in either hand,
a masked brigand
struts arrogantly up the road

Sakutarô adored flicks that featured bandits or villains.

I watch blue flames blaze on every living thing

Hallucinations terrorized Sakutarô as he struggled to convert his visions into words.

Look! Here he comes:
a silver wolf dashing at me from afar

This phantasmal work hints of untamed, chaotic and destructive primordial urges.

I personally thrashed myself

A month before this poem appeared, Sakutarô intensified his self-flagellation by making cold water lustration part of his daily penance. Pouring icy water over one's head, especially in winter, toughens both body and spirit. Sakutarô's objective was purgation of sin through acts of penance that might free his conscience of guilt—especially over his intense sexual longings. This is one sense of whipping or thrashing himself like a packhorse. Another consists of verbal lashings accomplished through his many poems of penitence.

NOTES FROM UNDERGROUND

I open the door to the waiting room. Sakutarô sits crumpled on the one chair. I stand and wait. He remains motionless, staring straight ahead. I walk to my chair behind the couch, leaving the doors to the waiting and consultation rooms open. Soon he shuffles in, looking immensely sad. Seeming almost puny, he gives off a glint of defiance. A wave of sadness sweeps over me.

My core yields radium. Oh, yes, I yield radium—a small, penetrating amount with no awe of any sun! Light of light, soul of soul, an atom of dynamism, the quintessence of science, the essence of sensitivity, the loveliest luminescence among all things lovely—that's what my core yields. Transparent crystal-like fireflies gleam throughout my body. Fireflies gleam.

He breathes in and out, audibly, trance-like. I work hard to keep my tools in working order—trying to maintain focus and openness despite feeling confused and pummeled. These competencies are my responsibility when, as Bion observed, a Scientific Conversation turns brutally intimate. I myself now feel exactly as does Sakutarô, a puny tyke standing up against blinding and overwhelming vastness—light of a giant sun, radioactivity. Against these indifferent forces, the two of us are trying to muster a pathetic defiance.

Sakutarô suddenly goes limp.

I now hear the newborns' ever so faint choruses coming from daybreak's distant horizon. At the portals of this earliest miracle I join my palms in prayer and shudder in ecstasy and in anguish.

Joining his palms over his chest, he shudders.

My mind clears. I tell him, "From the core of the woman's body, an interior as fecund as the sun and as mysterious as that of radioactive luminescence, emerge the choruses of the newborn. The miracle of a woman's body makes you shudder in ecstasy and anguish."

Oh, yes, that's the true configuration of my pathetic sensitivities.

Before I can say a word he shakes himself like a dog, snaps his head and bounds into a sitting position. He blinks repeatedly, as though trying to come to. He begins talking earnestly, rattling on with professorial efficiency.

The fact that we are alive means our feelings are animated. Feelings alone are true. Everything else is false: a mere delusion. Only works that feature sentiment are true poet-

ry, the art among arts. We create poetry so we can deal with feelings. There is no ideology in our art. In our art are only feelings. Sentiment is our all.

"Are you making a professional statement about your art?"

A look of slyness tugs Sakutarô's face.

Suddenly-swelled-up poppy seeds yield cocaine. Opium. Quinine.

"Thank you, that's helpful," I respond. "The drug world also insists feelings alone are true. What's the drug culture but an insistence on the primacy of feelings? I gather words are a drug."

His body tenses and his face darkens. He turns away.

Look!

he says, looking back at me again, his face hard.

Look! A splendid aurora borealis behind the penitent, hands clasped in prayer. An eternally moonless night sleeps and dreadful icebergs drift over the horizon. Ponder the drift of the ages, the jet blackness, the muted moments, the unitary dread of an individual suspended in space. Ponder his corpse's radiant soul.

"I suggest you ponder the issue of envy, which, I'm conjecturing, is filling you with murderous hate. You state that writing is the art of arts. You just spoke splendidly. 'Ponder the drift of the ages.' Wonderful. However, compared with the newborns' choruses, you judge your work mere fireflies despite all your bravura to the contrary. My core yields radium, you tell us. Radiant language. However, it does not yield babies. It does not create the earliest miracle of life. Each of us comes through the portal of a mother's body."

I do not change my gaze, but I don't stare at him, either. I stay busy thinking, now that I have my mind back. He leans forward, a hand on each knee. He looks straight at me.

A hound roams the graveyard on a moonlit night. This hound howls at Earth's distant core. The howling hound—*a human being*.

The tension evaporates. He recognizes me as a comrade-in-arms. I say wryly, "The flow of life will not be compromised by the howling of a dog."

This ashen hound paws impatiently at the packed soil because it intuits what stirs in that far, faraway subterranean realm. The howling hound agonizes, grows frantic and fidgets as it tries to dig up what directly confronts it in that depressing moonlit graveyard.

"Namely, that great forces of life and time lie concealed deep in the heart of the world. These are what gave you life."

You'll howl till a neighbor with a sick child guns you down.

"You're merely a writer who will get gunned down by time, landing in a graveyard while the story goes on forever."

The session ends, and he leaves. I want to laugh. I want to cry. Sakutarô's right on—my core and his yield radium. True, only a small, penetrating amount, yet it is the loveliest luminescence among all things lovely. We humans paw impatiently at the secrets of life, agonize, fidget, grow frantic, and most wonderfully howl with the miracle of language. Sakutarô has shared a sublime truth, and I am grateful.

NOTES FROM ABOVEGROUND

Crystal-like fireflies gleam throughout my body

Sakutarô associates fireflies with sensuous love. The light they emit, cool though it may be, he links with poetry and the passion inherent in every living being.

We create poetry so we can deal with feelings

That's the standard, time-honored Japanese approach to lyric writing. Essentially, it's also Sakutarô's blueprint for successful free verse. Wherever we look, we find him working to mold personal feelings and experiences into works of art. His definition of "feelings," so often darkly melancholic or twisted by testosterone, differs radically from conventional notions. Rather than focusing almost exclusively on love, nature-embedded imagery or romantic sentiments, he tells us how time, genes and instincts, how failures and losses, wound his psyche.

This ashen hound paws impatiently at the packed soil

Words like "ashen" suggest paleness and stand for the dog's—that is to say, for Sakutarô's—physical and psychic illnesses. The animal's impatient pawing mirrors the writer's instinct-driven attempts to get at the core of things, to penetrate the psyche, ideas Sakutarô borrowed from Nietzsche.

The powers of the psyche, in turn, can grasp realms invisible to the senses of ordinary people but inherently accessible to animals and to the intuitions of the artist. Whenever Sakutarô topples the idols of impersonal, nature-embedded statements, he gives Japan's literary gods the finger.

Session
Relentless Fecundity 11

NOTES FROM UNDERGROUND

Sakutarô does not show up for two weeks. He leaves no message. At the beginning of our work together, I set time aside for him, as requested. Unless informed otherwise, this time remains his, to do with as he pleases. If he chooses not to come, or leaves early, fine. His financial responsibility for the sessions remains a constant. He honored this arrangement when he tossed that crumpled check at me a while back. I make no effort to contact him. An absence, like a silence, can be as informative as any statement whispered or howled. Showing up after five missed sessions, Sakutarô appears emaciated and ill.

He says quietly,

When I peeped into the nest, I found it vaguely dim. It contained but a single grayish egg glowing somewhat ominously. Masses of a sickling's fine hair tangled together into balls all around it—a pile of truly countless hairs.

"Have you been ill?" I ask.

Tangled randomly in the nests, countless human hairs begin to tremble. On winter's first day, fine green roots begin to reach up from the ailing ground—they begin reaching up.

His voice is low and sad.

They seem truly pathetic, so wispy, so very, very pitiful.

"How different from Jesus telling his twelve disciples, 'Are not two sparrows sold for a farthing? And one of them shall not fall on the ground without your Father. But the very hairs of your head are all numbered.' This sickling, yourself, has countless hairs. You are as faceless as a mass of baby rats tangled together into balls. I suggest your recent illness made you feel truly pathetic. It provided ominous evidence you live in an indifferent universe."

The face of a wretched sickling emerges in the subterranean gloom.

He flings out both arms and roars,

Each day I became more sharply honed. My hands become brass. My fingertips utterly transformed into awls. I swell up like a snake that had just swallowed a frog.

"Despite your illness, you continued to write."

Aching everywhere, I twist and writhe in agony. I'll actually try to make cherry blossoms bloom in my festering innards. I'll have a radium moon sprout from my contaminated soul.

He begins to sob.

I shrivel. I waste away. Yes, my feet inch closer to the grave. Look! Clenching my teeth with frantic determination, I pray for that frightful final miracle.

Bitterly, his voice crackling with contempt, he says,

Bamboo root hairs push on like awls, dwindle into silky threads, then fade away like smoke.

"May I ask what's the frightful final miracle?"
Silence.
"I suggest the frightful final miracle is sanity. And by that I mean a reconciliation on your part with the facts of life—despite twisting and writhing because of your pathetic insignificance, your envy of birth and women's bodies and the stuff those lowlife romantic poets wrote about. Escaping from penance and the accursed fecundity of moral mania—I'm paraphrasing Immanuel Kant—that's miraculous."

His miseries multiply as his illness worsens. During the last three months of cloudy skies, bamboo has been reaching up from the sickling's contagion, reaching up from his shoulders, reaching up from his hand. Bamboo reaches up even from below his waist.

"You recognize sexual life is inexorably tied in with the relentless fecundity of the vast vegetative world."

Indeed, as the nests gloomily begin to blur, he so wastes away that everyone will of course pity him.

"Nature won't, of course. It multiplies without pity."

Hairs glowing like silk make his ordeal more and more poignantly unbearable until eventually he's stripped completely naked—all the while shrieking in anguish to his heart.

A long pause.

And still firmly attached to the bamboo roots, still grubbing, grubbing, grubbing for their root tips.

"The vegetative world is unbearably relentless—like sexual desire. You're stuck with desire as you're stuck with an illness. However, here's the miraculous. Despite all your shrieking you in fact attach yourself firmly to the bamboo roots, still grubbing, grubbing, grubbing for their root tips.

"You remain part of the living world despite the anguish sexual forces, indifferent and forever fecund, cause. Especially when laid low by illness, and realizing in your festering innards how vulnerable, for all your powers, you are."

He exhales audibly and lies quiet until the time ends. He seems exhausted but also at peace. He has fought the good fight and emerges sane. The two of us share a great victory.

NOTES FROM ABOVEGROUND

A pile of truly countless hairs

Hair suggests fertility and the dynamism of procreation. Monks traditionally shave their heads to symbolize their abandonment of sex.

The face of a wretched sickling emerges in the subterranean gloom

"Sick Subterranean Face" is one of the most famous and original works in the corpus. Sakutarô says he based this poem on the nightmare of having been buried alive.

Each day I became more sharply honed my hands become brass

An almost unbearable sharpening of emotions and sensitivity suggests mental disturbance. Brass, an alloy of copper and zinc, is "sham gold" and very hard. Sakutarô could have known the English usage of brass as bold self-assurance or audacity. "The Final Miracle's" title has as plausible referents the mysteries of conception, birth, and the absolution of sin.

Not many readers resist becoming almost sappily mesmerized by the endless loose ends, the delicious incongruities, the omnipresent chaos, and the vivid Polaroid shots that his writings present of his inner life. These characteristics of Sakutarô's work gravely eroded Japan's literary conventions and stand almost one hundred and eighty degrees opposed to traditional concerns for celebrating the inexhaustible loveliness and aliveness of nature or the ephemerality of beauty and life.

Session **12**

Finite Means, Infinite Purposes

NOTES FROM UNDERGROUND

Sakutarô misses the next session. As always, I use his time to mull. I think about the issue of "diagnosis." What's Sakutarô's problem? True, he'd been physically ill lately, a "sickling." However, that's not what joins us in conversation. Physicians work in a closed world, a quantitative one. Medicine is a normative science. A physician has a precise idea of what constitutes health—the numbers cranked out by blood analysis, respiratory volumes, the millisecond patterns of electrical cardiac impulses. If the numbers don't "fit" you're sick.

There are no "numbers," no exactly defined quantities, in the domain, Scientific Conversation. A capacity for language is what empowers the mind. "Language uses finite means for infinite purposes." The number of words in a dictionary is finite. The rules of syntax are finite. Conjoining these two finite quantities, mind generates sentences without number. Of the millions and millions of books in the Library of Congress, no two sentences read the same, unless directly quoted. Our power to create sentences without number out of two sets of precisely numbered elements—vocabulary and grammar—is our glory. Of course we can't say anything meaningful without words and syntax, but they can't ever tell us what to say. We have leaped into another world, the universe of discourse. We'll create sentences until doomsday and nothing can stop us from creating fresh ones. This infinite fecundity demonstrates the quintessence of mind, its creativity and originality.

Grant that Hagiwara Sakutarô is a unique and unrepeatable human being. Each of us is, likewise, especially evident when we start talking. At the same time, we're all much more human than otherwise. We belong to the same species and have for tens of thousands of years. Sakutarô is not from Mars. I've met him before. So have Freud and Klein and Bion. I find it exhilarating that Sakutarô talks like someone who walked off the street in Vienna or Los Angeles. He struggles with hatred for life, with envy of the mother, with incalculable conflicts about sex. What's great fun is that through language I get to know him without violating his uniqueness. That is what talking together makes possible. Isaiah instructed the people to listen to the word of the Lord. The great prophet claimed the Lord had had it with burnt offerings, the fat of fed beasts, the blood of bullocks and lambs and goats. "I am weary to bear them." Instead, the Lord says, "Come now and let us reason together."

Sakutarô and I are happily doing the work of Isaiah's Lord. Are Sakutarô's problems better thought of as religious rather than sexual? Is Freud and Klein's emphasis on the death instinct better conceptualized as original sin? The Church Fathers pushed the line, "In sin did my mother conceive me." Is that what the lamentable history of the

Catholic Church toward sex is about, the death instinct? A murderous attack against life? I bump into this mind problem in every Scientific Conversation. It can be terrifying. It is inexplicable.

I have no idea as to its provenance. The idea of a death instinct, like that of original sin, may border on the quaint—Thanatos pitted against Eros—concepts unpalatable to our scientific sensibilities. No doubt, however, the phenomenon is real.

In my judgment, Wilfred Bion has come up with the best phenomenological description of the mind problem—we humans suffer from mental skin that is too thin. We are penetrated violently by the imperfections of the world. We are forever disappointed. Our existence gives offense!

Session
What's Below the Waist
13

NOTES FROM UNDERGROUND

Sakutarô arrives ten minutes early, switching on from the waiting room a light in my office signaling his arrival. I am eager to see him. My eagerness tips me off. I am having counter-transference—as it is called in the field—and my responsibility is to recognize it. I wait to start the session on time. Despite his genius, Sakutarô suffers from incredible envy of sexual life and creativity. If he can imagine himself The Good Breast—by my rushing out to bring him in early—there goes the ball game.

My counter-transference would enable Sakutarô to fantasize he possesses all the goodies, and I can't wait to get my hands on them. Good-by problems with rivalry and envy coming to life in our relationship. His ordinariness is the focus of our work, not his genius. One aspect of his greatness, of course, is his ability to make the ordinary accessible.

He appears ill. Washed out. Lifeless.

A frog in alcohol. A rat in alcohol. A heart in alcohol. Shellfish in alcohol.

"You look pickled. Are you?"
He responds by becoming completely colloquial.

Around 3 a.m. Walking this way from down the street: a patrolman. Walking here: the drunken poet. "Hey you! Where ya goin'?" "To buy a woman." "Moron!"

"Isn't the patrolman asking, 'What are you doing to yourself?'"

I'm standing on the bridge, my mind a blank. Tepid water flows beneath me.

"I'm guessing you feel so bad about your behavior you have thoughts of jumping off the bridge into the water below."

It's around 3 a.m. Moon glows vaguely gray in the sky. A fellow dangling a red watch-lantern comes my way. "Who are ya?" "I'm a human being." "Blockhead! I'm askin' yer name." "My name is Hagiwara." "Where's yer home?" "Maebashi." "You idiot! What part?" "Kuruwa Machi." "Humph." Unfortunately, spring stood behind us jeering.

"A frog, a rat, a shellfish—these have no name. They say, 'You've seen one drunk you've seen 'em all.'"
Sakutarô says nothing for a few minutes.

A seductive night. Two jet-black cats on the roof. A

thread-like sliver of a crescent moon looming hazily over the tips of their upright tails.

He then says, unmistakably in the universal phonology of seduction,

Owa—**Good evening.**

"I gather that's the first cat."

Owa—**Good evening.**

"Okay, now we've got the second cat."

Ogya—Ogya—Ogya.

"I get the picture."
Bitterly he replies,

The head of this house is sick.

"You head up your life—but as your own worst enemy."

This morning I had too many helpings of cabbage,

he retorts dismissively and falls silent.
Almost audibly I catch my breath. Freud had stunned the world with his *Three Essays on Sexuality*, demonstrating that sexual life involves the entire body and not just genitals. Melanie added immeasurably to his work by linking body zones and body functions, above all urethral and evacuatory, with aggressive fantasies. I break the silence. "May I ask what you're thinking?"
He responds in a rage.

Why stand there gaping at me? And why snicker so grotesquely? Oh, of course, if it's a matter of what's below my waist, well, it's somewhat ridiculous, but you know that for sure is why I'm standing indoors by the window on this ashen wall.

"You can protect yourself easily enough from the embarrassment of flatulence, from eating cabbage, by standing indoors alone. What makes you snicker grotesquely is that below your waist your sexual and evacuatory powers are as closely conjoined as in a rat or a frog.

"'Who are you?' asks the patrolman. Obviously an animal, with animal physiology. A problem arises in that you are also a human being. All that's below your waist as well as above has to be gathered together under a single name. When you denude the complexity of human sexual life by alcohol, or buying a nameless woman, or contemptuously likening it to two cats going at it, you recognize in the person of the patrolman you are besmirching your person and your place in this world. You liken it to the behavior of a blockhead, but recognizing this problem is not the same as changing it. That task is what brings you here again."

He does not respond but does not leave until time is up. Life has flowed back into Sakutarô. Astonishingly, he no longer looks hung over. I think of Melanie Klein's seminal work on early mental life. Sakutarô describes as vividly as Melanie fantasied attacks against The Good Breast through body products. No surprise, really. Doesn't colloquial speech inexhaustibly refer to body parts and body products in striving for vividness?

NOTES FROM ABOVEGROUND

During this time, Sakutarô, age twenty-nine, published almost thirty poems dealing with his continued attempts to expiate his sins and lighten his conscience.

A heart in alcohol

Even before his late twenties, Sakutarô had become such a heavy and constant drinker that he was surely on the way to becoming as pickled as the contents of those jars.

Kuruwa Machi

The patrolman abandons his haughtiness on hearing Sakutarô name Kuruwa Machi, which he knew to be an upper-class neighborhood. Throughout the Tokugawa era (1615-1868), all cities—especially castle towns, of which Maebashi was one—prescribed which part of town each social class might reside in. Generally speaking, samurai lived closest to, the despised merchants farthest from, the castle.

Unfortunately, spring stood behind us jeering

Spring jeers because it's universally been the time for orgies—dancing round the Maypole—and spring's sybaritic indulgences. For Sakutarô, spring is always the time when hormones and horniness get the upper hand.

Owa—Ogya

These meaningless sounds, Sakutarô's inventions, mean to mimic the cat.

Notes from Underground

Sakutarô does not show up for three weeks. After the seventh missed session I drop him a note. "I am keeping your sessions unless instructed otherwise." Three days later, after another missed session, I receive a letter. It is the first of the month, and his fee is due. The letter contains a check for the monies owed for the full month—the check not crumpled or wrinkled this time. I am pleased.

Nice to have that sense of closure the calendar and payment afford. Nice to think Sakutarô has the emotional wherewithal to continue our conversations. The next day he shows up, forty-five minutes late.

He comes in, lies down and says,

There's a sickling in the room.

Yeah, I think to myself, also a gunslinger at high noon.

We're gonna have us a shoot-out. My dear partner, I think to myself, you miss three weeks. You pay the previous month's bill in full. You arrive today, still physically sick, with five minutes left of the session. What do I do? Extend the time? Make magical allowance?

I say out loud, "I presume the sickling in the room is you."

His house is made of aluminum. Its windows are definitely triangular. Snow had been falling on the house. Pale blossoms bloom on cherry trees. Pathetic glass fragments lie scattered everywhere over the floor.

"Are the glass fragments from broken bottles of booze?"

A metal chair sits in the rented upstairs room. On the roof a napping black cat.

Time is up. I state, "We have to stop here." He gets up and leaves with nary a backward glance. I tell myself, "Well, the sun is 800,000 miles in diameter. Our Big Ben in the sky. If I think I can slow it down for a couple minutes, giving extra time to Sakutarô, I'm really crazy. We had used up our five minutes. That's it. Check with the sun."

Keeping time and money straight between us says something very powerfully to Sakutarô about me. "I'm sane. I don't think I am bigger than life. I submit to its strictures like everyone else." Wilfred called this kind of communication "the language of achievement," a phrase he borrowed from John Keats. True, every sentence we speak is freshly minted, and this inventiveness is inexhaustible. Nonetheless, ultimately our little lives are rounded by a sleep. We come full circle, with a beginning and an end. We are finite creatures. We get born, and we die at some point. Subjecting time and money to arithmetic makes this great truth a palpable achievement in conversational work. Unless I speak the language of achievement as surely as I compute two plus two make four, I lose all credibility.

Notes from Aboveground

His house is made of aluminum.
Its windows are definitely triangular

These lines, from an unpublished verse in the Notebooks, describe impressions of a "House Viewed on a Moonlit Night." Moonlight glittering on aluminum—a material not then used in building houses—hints at a surrealistic scene. It is difficult to imagine a house with triangular windows, but then moonlight is known (like sickness) to distort one's observations. In China, the triangle is a "female symbol," possibly by association with the pubic triangle; it may also indicate underworld powers. Pointing up, a triangle can imply escape or aspirations; space within the sides is seen as the common hearth. In those days, it was as original as it was daring to use words like "aluminum" and "triangular" in a poem. Among other objections, such words are definitely not "poetic."

Pale blossoms bloom on cherry trees

This image sets the poem in spring, the season when hormones run amuck and people enjoy themselves by dancing and drinking under cherry trees in bloom. Paleness links with the sickling and emphasizes how sad he must be feeling incapacitated at this time of the year. Spring in conjunction with sickness and moonlight (and the lunacy associated with the moon) tends to emphasize the surreal or uncanny essence of this scene.

A metal chair sits in the rented upstairs room

The figure of a rented room with a metal chair contains a touch of the exotic. At the very least, most readers in those days would connect this image either with a Western city or at least a large metropolitan area. Metal for Sakutarô relates to what is modern, urban, and manly; it also stands for the libido—solidified life energy. An empty chair could possibly suggest the absence of authority.

Session
Rats Making Nests
15

NOTES FROM UNDERGROUND

As Sakutarô comes into the office, he pointedly makes eye contact with me as he walks by. Remarkably, he appears importunate. He says he is going to...

give a report from my cell.

For what seems forever, however, he reports nothing. Then,

Bit by bit spring brings its torments; this convalescent's breathing becomes an agony; rats' nests have honeycombed the attic of his cell. Rats making nests. Rats making nests.

I respond, "Rats making babies. Rats making babies."

The gloomy area above my ceiling swarms with ash-hued house rats. They've built their nests there. Entangled woven nests, entangled nests. Yes, rip off my ceiling boards and you'll find rats' nests here, there—everywhere.

"Sexual goings on. Here, there, everywhere."

Look!

he shouts out sharply. He points a finger at the ceiling and waits for me to reply.

"Rip off my ceiling boards and help me with my torments, you plead. 'I'm reporting from the ceiling of my mind. Pay attention to its workings."

All day long my pale and sickly shadow-like flesh enters and leaves my cell through this massive door. I fade away like a ghost.

"Massive door?" I muse aloud. "My guess is you're proposing to shut off your five senses."

The cherry trees are blooming, but instead of going out to view them I spend the entire day at prayer.

"Yes. When you remove yourself from the sensible world, from life in your own body as registered through the senses, you fade away like a ghost."

I'm only aware that the bloodstained tails of living things skim at times over my soul. Those instants of light are truly miraculous.

"How did you put it the other day? 'At the portals of this

earliest miracle...'" He doesn't let me finish.

I join my palms in prayer and shudder in ecstasy and in anguish. Oh, yes, that's the true configuration of my pathetic sensitivities.

"In the middle of your prayers, the bloodstained tails of birthing rats skim over your soul. You shudder in ecstasy and in anguish. The swarming fecundity of the world shapes the true configuration of your pathetic sensitivities. The problem is you can't win for losing. Sensitivity underlies your powers but also causes maddening entanglements in the ceiling of your mind."

I don't know the answer yet. I don't know why rats' nests honeycomb my ceiling. I know only that I'm simply concentrating on that silk-like something that forever dangles from the index finger of my left hand.

"You write unceasingly. Alas, the subject matter for your work, it turns out, concerns sex. And that drives you crazy."

I must grit my teeth and pray till my lips turn blue. From morning till night, flames in my gas stove burn pallidly blue. They cast on the walls of my cell the shadows of ever more dreadful creatures.

"You pray, until your lips turn blue, to protect you from seeing the bloody business of birthing by these living things."

He lies silent for a long time, eyes wide open.

Ah, rats making nests. The attic of my cell now jet black with them.

"Rats keep making nests in your mind. You keep your eyes open to the facts of life."

My malady turns increasingly pallid. I fail.

"Your sanity succeeds in overriding every attempt you make to escape biology through prayer."

Sakutarô closes his eyes and again lies quiet. Has he fallen asleep? I interject, "May I ask what you're thinking?"

Cherry trees begin to bloom brightly; to watch them is to dream of lands beyond the sea.

"You can't have one without the other—the brightly blooming cherry trees and the swarming jet black rats. Rats make babies, cherry trees make blossoms."

Leaving, he smiles at me, at least for the moment healed. Bion never tired of pointing out that sex is an unknown. So puzzling. Sakutarô experiences the coming of spring with its renewal of life an unbearable agony. The Church Fathers railed against sex. *Mirabile dictu*—they claimed birthing a child makes a woman unclean. Babies make humans "no longer different from the pigs," asserted St. Jerome. Why does life in the body engender such hostility? Why is celibacy superior to marriage? Jesus is born of a virgin, also immaculately conceived? Why is sex maculate?

David Hume pointed out that the process of naming establishes a constant conjunction. It puts under one roof, as it were, any number of elements. Bion used the term sex as a constant conjunction. Freud established that sex includes erotogenic zones, elements that enormously broadened the phenomenon. In this session Sakutarô makes evident prayer is an element conjoined by the term sex. And most vividly, so is agony.

Notes from Aboveground

Sakutarô published these poems between the ages of twenty-eight and thirty. While writing them he suffered from a medley of ailments: gonorrhea, hemorrhoids, intestinal problems, and depression.

Rats making nests

For this poet—if not for the rats—the torments of spring, which can begin in February, are primarily sexual. Rats associate with fertility and plague, and have often been associated with the most repugnant aspects of the human soul or with misfortune. The conned persona may, moreover, have in mind the Chinese folk concept of rats as fiendish male figures juxtaposed to female fox demons intent on devouring them. Nest could as well mean "love nest."

Rip off my ceiling boards

The ceilings of traditional Japanese homes are not made of plaster or acoustic tiles but of thin unpainted wooden boards with visible grain markings. This makes them aesthetically pleasing and conveys warmth. At the same time, natural wooden ceiling boards make a room quite gloomy because they reflect little light.

Cherry trees begin to bloom brightly, to watch them is to dream of lands beyond the sea

Cherry blossoms link, like the Maypole, with riotous if not orgiastic enjoyments that nobody invited Sakutarô to join. In Japan, these blossoms have since ancient days been metaphors for ephemerality—like an orgasm. If he lived abroad among people with his values they would let him join in celebrating spring. Meanwhile he feels miserably lustful.

NOTES FROM UNDERGROUND

When I open the door to the waiting room, I star-tle. Sakutarô sees my reaction and smiles with a hint of triumph. He is wearing a chapeau, blue gloves, and twirling his familiar cane. He also wears lipstick, his face touched with rouge, and white powder daubed on his neck. He strolls in grandly, props his cane in a corner, takes time to remove gloves and chapeau, and lies down on the couch. Watching, I remember his importunate glance the session before.

The substance of spring,

he announces.
   "I'm all ears."

Countless insect eggs have made spring swell firmly.

He speaks with a lilt to his voice.

If you look very, very carefully you're sure to see such eggs crammed everywhere you can think of. Eggs have been laid everywhere over every surface: even, for example, on the delicate wings of moth-like creatures—thus the glistening dazzle of their wings.

"You talk like a biologist."

Ah, these inconspicuous oblong eggs invisible to the naked eye contend everywhere with each other for space.

"Now you talk like the great biologist Darwin, who recognized natural selection operates on numberless eggs crammed into every niche and laid everywhere over every surface. Sex makes the world go round."

Let me tell you what's on my mind. I long for a woman. I crave a woman. Bleary-eyed with passion, I'm ready to risk my all.

"You're willing to risk everything for a sexual relationship. Woman occupies every niche of your mind She is all you think of. She covers you everywhere, even over every nook and cranny of your body."
He sits up and faces me, smiling broadly.

I reddened my lips and kissed the fresh bark of a white birch. Even supposing I were a handsome fellow, I have no rubber-ball breasts. Nor have I the scent of smooth powder on my skin. I'm just a shriveled-up, ill-starred male. Oh, what a pathetic fellow!

"If you're supposed to look like a beautiful woman, I agree."

Today in a stand of dazzling trees on this fragrant May-time field, I slipped neatly into sky-blue gloves, wrapped my hips with a makeshift corset, and daubed my neck with white makeup.

"That's how much you crave a woman."

Then, bending my head back a bit, as young girls do, I kissed the trunk of a sapling birch. Already twenty-eight, my longing to hold a woman drove me to tightly embrace one of those blazing trees.

He sits back on the couch. Tears flow down his cheek. In a whisper he says mournfully,

My heart blazes with youthful élan, but though I pray through tears, character flaws rob me of all good things.

He stands up, gathers his gloves and chapeau, and bows. He announces this as our last session. Again, I give an involuntary startle. "Whatever you say."

He pauses at the door.

Will life always be like this?

"We'll talk about it next time."
He sharply reminds me this is our last session.
"We'll talk about it next time."
He leaves abruptly, slamming the door behind him. I don't expect to see him again. I feel sick. Furious and deeply sad. The game was on! In the middle of it he quits. It's the

one sin I can't forgive a partner: Counter-transference, no doubt. Who cares! He picked up his toys and went home. I hate him.

For comfort I reflect on Melanie Klein's *Envy and Gratitude.* I remember Bion describing the work of Scientific Conversation as a response to the inappropriate. Didn't Sakutarô show up dressed wonderfully inappropriately? Thinking like Darwin and talking like an angel. And then he quits! I want to choke him! I mull the battle of the sexes, a war simply too much for him. That's his character flaw. That's what robs him of all good things. And he robbed both of us by breaking off our rousing conversation. I feel miserable.

Notes from Aboveground

Countless eggs have made spring swell firmly

In identifying eggs as the essence of spring, Sakutarô feminizes the season. This helps make the juxtaposed "swell firmly" resonate with tumescence. Egg-covered cherry blossoms is a repulsive figure; equating the mica-like glints on moth wings with ova is equally odd. To suggest that apprehending spring's true nature requires tactile as well as visual engagement enables the persona to make an end run around conventional ways to appreciate, evaluate or describe this season.

I reddened my lips

Censors said that depicting a man in drag would corrupt public morals and forced Sakutarô to excise this poem from the collection. They ignored his complaint that passages from the Song of Solomon in the Bible and ancient Japanese poetry collections were far more "corrupting." Rouge, lipstick and corsets serve as vehicles of transformation, but in the poet's milieu they are distinctly exotic or foreign female accouterments. They do, however, enable him to metamorphose from a bohemian dandy into a woman (here a professional) whom he longs to possess. By doing so, he hopes, perhaps, to diminish his frustrations over not having a sexual partner and a woman to fuss over and indulge him.

Daubed my neck with white makeup

This denotes that Sakutarô intends masquerading as a woman in the entertainment industry. Such women specialize in titillating men and making them feel "manly."

I kissed the trunk of a sapling birch

Trees can be objects of sexual desire because they display incredible reproductive vigor in their annual spring rebirth. As such, they can easily serve as symbols of the life force or Eros. Birch, used for the phallic Maypole, has long had an erotic sense. Birch rods were also effective for expelling demons, witches and various evil spirits.

Hagiwara Sakutarô, 1919

PART II

The Human Trinity

NOTES FROM UNDERGROUND

As I leave my office one Monday night early in April, a darkened figure emerges out of the shadows. I give a start and then recognize Sakutarô. He looks bedraggled and vaguely ill. He insists he has to talk to me immediately, if only for fifteen minutes. It's an emergency.

"There are no emergencies," I tell myself, trying to get my bearings. Bion observed every work has its own time-scale. An ordinary and obvious fact of life. Astronomers had 5000 years to solve the problem of the planets, from the Babylonians to Newton and Einstein; paramedics have five minutes to solve the problem of cardiac arrest. Getting a job done requires thinking, which is nigh impossible when bombarded by the catastrophic.

I feel blind sided! If I don't see Sakutarô immediately, I fail to recognize the severity of his suffering. If I do, how do I deal with his violent intrusion without giving a sense of panic and collapse? "I need to be taken in, now!" Melanie observed the infant screaming in terror. "I am dying." And The Good Breast gathers in the burning bits and pieces, detoxifies and reassembles them in its cool and comforting ensconcement, healing the child.

"I am dying!" Sakutarô shouts at me in the darkened hall. "Help me! Help me!"

But I can't help him if I become overwhelmed by his terrors and lose all capacity to think. "Do something," his brightly glimpsed eyes implore me. I feel pressure building in my chest. Leaning on Bion and Klein, I take a deep breath and simply stand and wait, mulling the situation. My head clears.

I unlock the waiting room door I had just locked, turn on the light, and ask him to take a seat. I go into my office and for a brief instant again try to gather my thoughts. I decide further delay will make matters only worse. The time to deal with the work is now. I go back to the waiting room and tell him I'll meet with him for fifteen minutes.

He goes straight to the couch! Immediately I suggest he sit in a chair rather than using the couch. He stops and looks straight at me. I watch the terror evaporate from his eyes. All pressure leaves my chest. He feels protected and comforted. His assault on our structure, driven by the catastrophic, has been contained by the simple act of my asking him to use a chair and not the couch. He hadn't set up an appointment. We hadn't met for at least a year. Suddenly Bam! he explodes out of a darkened hallway.

"Let's first get our bearings," I tell him.

When he sits down, he looks healed. It has all happened in a moment, in the twinkling of an eye. The work has taken less than a minute. Plenty of time.

I strolled the dry channel of the river that flows by

Maebashi feeling unimaginably downcast.

"Is that what brings you here? You're drying up and want to resume our conversations?"

Directly in front of where I crouched motionless in the riverbed grew a clump of channel *yomogi*. As though to snatch my soul, my hand reached swiftly into the clump and plucked something resembling dried-up hair: a skylark nest concealed in the *yomogi*.

"Our skylark returns!" I say brightly, cheered by the realization the work is going well. "Last I heard you cooked the skylark and roasted the romantic poets."
He replies, in lilting cadence,

The parent larks called from the sky: *piyo-piyo-piyo-piyo-piyo-piyo-piyo-piyo*. I had the clear sense of being charmed by the love of something tenderly cared for.

"Both parent larks singing. Hail to thee, blithe spirits! Then why are you in such an agitated state?"

Four gray skylark eggs glistened cheerlessly in the nest's dim light. I reached out and picked one up. Life's warm throb tingled the tip of my thumb. When I held the egg gently to the sunlight and looked through it, I noticed a pale red shape vaguely resembling a clot. Then I sensed something like juice cooling my skin—a raw smelling fluid trickled between my fingers. The egg was broken! Merciless human fingers had crushed its delicate shell.

Suddenly overcome with grief, he says,

I'd broken the egg. I'd slain love and joy, a deed ripe with distress and damnation, an act both dismal and disagreeable.

He weeps silently.

I became absorbed in brooding about things I find loathsome: People who detest the smell of others. People who find the genitals repulsive. Those who hate others.

I say nothing. He is saying it all.

I adore yet dread people. I confess. I confess my sin.

Tears streaming down his face, he looks directly at me, brow furrowed, eyes narrowed.

Spring erupts like smallpox from the soil.

Softly and after a long pause, he adds,

How compassionately I'd picked up the lark's egg.

"You link smallpox and a lark's egg. I suggest what brings you here tonight is that your loving ends in murder."

Sakutarô gets up, takes a tissue, and wipes his eyes before opening the door and leaving. I stay in my chair a long time, staggered by the evening's experience. In those last two sentences he had penetrated to the heart of Freud and Klein and Bion—Eros and Thanatos. What has happened to our lipstick, rouge and powder-patted fellow from a year ago? How cavalierly he had boasted, "Then, bending my head back a bit, as young girls do, I kissed the trunk of a sapling birch. Already twenty-eight, my longing to hold a woman drove me to tightly embrace one of those blazing trees."

Why had he then run? Tonight he tells us—because of overwhelming pain. He was threatened by a dreadful truth that took him a year to find the courage to speak. "I'd broken the egg. I'd slain love and joy, a deed ripe with distress and damnation, an act both dismal and disagreeable."

Over and over rang out in my head his mournful cry, "I became absorbed in brooding about things I find loathsome: People who detest the smell of others. People who find the genitals repulsive. Those who hate others."

Sakutarô is very fortunate. He loves The Breast. He loves woman. He longs for her above all else. And yet, he slays love and joy. He detests the smell of people, like Lear noting that Gloucester "smells of mortality." Sakutarô finds genitals repulsive for their inexhaustible fecundity. He is deeply driven and torn by love and hate simultaneously. Unless Sakutarô can reconcile these opposite states, he will carry out deeds ripe with damnation.

Eros and Thanatos. Call them what you will. Sakutarô finds these forces fundamental to the workings of his mind. Their colossal colliding threatens to hurl him into bottomless damnation.

NOTES FROM ABOVEGROUND

Background: Sakutarô issued no verse between September 1915 and May 1916, when "Lark's Nest" appeared. Emotionally and spiritually depressed, he claimed that when he wrote "Lark's Nest" he was at the depths of self-disgust and loathing. Only after writing it and realizing how cruel and hateful a person he was did he experience a rebirth. *Yomogi* for many Japanese elicits warm thoughts of mother's cooking and meals around the family table.

In October, Sakutarô had formed a mandolin club, which he directed. A mandolin would be nearly as exotic in provincial Maebashi as a samisen in Podunk, Iowa. In January 1916, the club performed its first concert in town. The following April Sakutarô organized Saturday seminars for local poets and musicians who examined the relation between verse and music. That spring he identified Nietzsche, Dostoyevsky and Poe as the primary influences on his work and thought.

Scholars comment negatively on the raw, unpolished nature of the language and the scatter-shot organization of "Lark's Nest." Language aside, however you look at it this poem is one of the most astonishing pieces in Sakutarô's corpus.

NOTES FROM UNDERGROUND

Two weeks after our "emergency" session, Sakutarô drops me a note. He wants to resume the work. I am to please let him know when time is available. A week later we begin afresh. As he comes into the consultation room, Sakutarô points to the chair I suggested he use a few weeks back, opening his hands and smiling slyly. He awaits my instructions. I tell him he may sit wherever he wants, except on my lap. I feel tickled. I had made the right move three weeks earlier, maintaining structure even during an "emergency." As usual, Wilfred had it straight—there are no emergencies.

One job needs to get done in a different time frame from another, that's all, from thousands of years to less than a minute. Asking Sakutarô to use the chair spoke The Language of Achievement, and for the two of us that means protecting him and me, the Conversational Couple, by keeping money and time straight. Or more subtly, maintaining the boundaries of our workbench despite screaming sirens and flashing red lights howling "Emergency! Emergency!" Melanie observed that growth and development depend on both structuring and vitalizing capacities provided by both parents. She employed the metaphor of The Good Breast and The Good Nipple, the latter analagous in its erectile and protecting powers to The Good Penis.

These powers are not the exclusive province of one sex or the other. A mother has structuring powers, a father vitalizing powers. Martin Buber asserted that love makes the other person present. Shaping this statement in the conceptual framework of projective identification, The Good Breast makes The Good Penis more vitalizing, The Good Penis makes The Good Breast more structuring. In plain English, a loving woman makes a good man a better woman, and a loving man makes a good woman a better man.

Sakutarô goes to the couch and lies down.

Is the person asleep under that chair the progeny of someone capable of begetting an enormous clan?

I have a guess about that chair.
He waits and then says,

The child wanted a flute. Thinking that his father would be writing in his study, the child peeked into his room and then stood silently by the door. From there he could see cherry blossoms shimmering.

"That chair," I offer. "Hmmm. I suggest you're also referring to that chair, right here, in this office. The one I recommended you use a couple weeks ago. That's what fathers do—maintain law and order. Three weeks ago we had parent larks, and now we get father himself, who shows up for the first time in our conversations. When you peeked into the lark's nest, disaster struck. Now, however, you peek into the father's study, wanting a flute, and beyond him you see cherry blossoms. I suggest you bring father together with mother, who is lovely as shimmering blossoms. A year ago, you came rouged, powdered, corseted; confusion reigned. Today you tell us the child lies asleep under the father's chair, secure and at peace. You want to once more play your flute and link the bestowal of your flute to the creative powers of both parents. You are not magically embodying father with your brandished cane and mother with your rouged face and corseted body."

The grownup in the room was deep in thought. The child noticed that the grownup had put his head on the desk.

I interject, "How observant the child is, how carefully it pays attention to the father."
Sakutarô shakes his head, giving a deep sigh.

Something that occurred this spring-like morning had saddened him. Feelings and reason. Oh, what misery for the adult who wants to separate emotion from logic!

His voice drops to a hush. I can scarcely hear him.

Breathless with fear, the grownup began to pray. "God! Don't let reason and feelings merge!"

Pause.

There stood the man's sallow, sickly child. The boy want-

ed a flute. He entered and stood in a corner of the room. Father's huge head bent low over his desk by the window. An enormous shadow stretched near his head. The child's gaze lit like a fly on that shadow.

Now whispering.

Something had bewitched the child's desolate heart. Gradually he began to feel his energies return. Then he let out a sharp cry. See that!

I practically jump out of my chair.

—a flute lying on the desk, the little purple flute he'd been longing for!

I am wonderfully gladdened. He has taken a giant step toward sanity. He accredits the sexual parents for his marvelous gifts as an artist. Alas, before I can savor this great accomplishment for even a moment he waves his hand as sharply as he had snapped,

See that!

And in a bored voice tosses out,

The child hadn't said a word to his father about the flute.

He stifles a yawn.

In truth, this was random luck, a matter of chance.

I shout, "Hold on a minute. I suggest it wasn't random luck at all. I suggested you use that chair the other week. You did not write for a year, landed back on my couch dried up and desolate."

He began to feel his energies return,

he repeats flippantly.

"You can't say it plainer than that," I holler back.

He waves me off.

Perhaps it was simply a wondrous stroke of good fortune. The child nonetheless believed that his father had performed a miracle: this grandest of grownups had produced that shadowy flute—that flute on the desk.

"It was simply a wondrous stroke of good fortune having nothing to do with you that your translator suggested you come talk with me. It was wondrous good fortune having nothing to do with you that Freud and Klein and Bion spent a lifetime trying to make sense out of your difficulties. It was a wondrous stroke of good fortune your folks married and, against all odds, you got born. I chose to have you sit on that chair. The father chose to give you a flute and support your gifts. You have very mixed feelings about accrediting mere ordinary folks for contributing so vitally to your existence because of decisions they made and not because of specialness on your part."

I am cranked. "You'd rather believe, naw, it's not a mere dad or mom, a hard-working translator or conversational partner. It's a miracle. Ol' Pops had nothing to do with the kid's flute. It was random luck. Mere chance. Maybe the Lord!" He gets up and storms out. I shout after him, "For God's sake, don't let reason and feelings merge!"

He never looks back.

Then it hits me. I drop my head and feel as defeated as that fantasied father Sakutarô just talked about. I had lost my bearings. The fine work we had accomplished together with the "chair" probably got undone by my impatience with his perverse ways and rivalrous attacks. Hell is the truth seen too late. I am forlorn. I cast about for comfort. I remind myself it sounds easy to do this work until you try it.

What had triggered my blundering anger? "Stop the guilt nonsense so you can think!" I shout out loud. I drift over the session and especially those brief fifteen minutes the session before. It was going oh so splendidly, Sakutarô growing by leaps and bounds and and aren't we on the glory road.

I remember Freud stressing the importance of working through. Rome wasn't built in a day. Try building brain structures that enable you to do the calculus. Takes huge effort and forever to do that. This work proposes to change a personality, after twenty-eight years in Sakutarô's case at the moment. Maybe it's presumptuous to undertake something on that scale. Bion said we come into the story very late. I remember that, too. Herbert Rosenfelt, who worked with Melanie and Wilfred for years, gave a series of seminars describing his work with a woman as envious and rivalrous as Sakutarô. Conversational work in its ninth year; five get-togethers weekly. Each session Rosenfelt reported featured splendid work. The problem was that the next session found her back at Square One.

"Once more unto the breach, dear friends." Surely Rosenfelt lacked something in his personality. That's what I believed until I tried it. What just happened with Sakutarô and me? Of course I should have done better—shouting and yelling after him like that. Embarrassing. What kind of worker worth his salt carries on like that? Fine, prattle on about counter-transference. Maybe I need another analysis. Or how about me trying a different line of work. *Mea culpa.*

The fact is, for all my limitations, I'm not the problem. The problem is the work goes too well. Sakutarô can't win for losing.

Peel the onion. Peel the onion. Peel the onion. Patience. Patience. Patience.

Notes from Aboveground

**See that—a flute lying on the desk,
the little purple flute he'd been longing for!**

Why a purple flute? The color may signify royalty or sensuality. The flute, of course, signifies poet or artist. For years Sakutarô had implored his conservative father to recognize him as a poet and concede that writing free verse was an honorable activity. That miracle never occurred.

Notes from Underground

As I open the door to the waiting room, Sakutarô bursts past me as though I don't exist. Rather than going to the couch or a chair, he prowls about the room. He holds a cane with a silver tip. He is wearing gloves. He wanders to the window and taps nervously on it with his gloved fingers. He grimaces repeatedly as though experiencing sharp pains.

My fortunes have changed drastically since yesterday—I wonder why. Surely the cherry trees will bud today and the Toné will endlessly flow.

"Nothing's changed in the outside world, but you've changed. Your agitation suggests it's a change for the worse."
He continues tapping.

Tomorrow we cannot meet, so how shall we get together the day after that?

"We won't. It's the weekend. Tomorrow's Saturday, the day after, Sunday. From my point of view, your fortunes have changed for the better. You recognize your need to be here. You dread the weekend which separates you from our work together."

Sakutarô stops tapping and stares out the window, every muscle tensed. Like a nun breathless with adoration I watch him, teetering on the brink of what Melanie Klein conceptualized as The Depressive Position. He hungers. He needs. He longs for. He is glimpsing what Melanie conceptualized as The Good Breast, and he mourns its approaching loss, the weekend, when he's on his own.

Sakutarô gives no hint he's heard a word I said. He remains motionless. I ask what he's thinking. No answer. I remember his fantasy of the purple flute. No sooner did he recognize it as a gift from the father than Sakutarô resorted to triumphalism and contempt. A fantasy evoked those violent responses. I'm sitting in the same room with him. The weekend loss brings his need and vulnerability to life right here on my lap. How to make them manageable before he explodes and God knows what.

I offer, "One of my mentors said that if one tries this work, there should be two rather frightened people in the room together. I suggest your realization of the weekend as something you'll miss scares you. In some unknown way." No answer.

I venture, "On the face of it, that you might miss coming here doesn't seem that disturbing." He turns his head sharply and glares at me. "Or troublesome. You wouldn't be here in the first place if our talking together didn't offer something of value. We have to wonder why...." He clears his throat loudly. I stop in mid-sentence.

He stretches out his cane, pointing it directly at me. He announces,

Satirical Poem—To my Ningyoshisha colleagues....

Sakutarô makes an ugly face, hinting at cruelty and violence, as does the pointed cane. He marches to the center of the room, keeping me in his sights.

My friend addressed his lice with an exceptionally contorted grimace. Hey, lice! For pity sake, don't congregate on me. You're truly gross. Stop plaguing me.

He leans toward me and says with mock solemnity,

This friend never once reached for an itch—a true sage.

He drops to his knees and begins pawing the carpet. His bizarreness puts me on edge.

Pushing aside the soil, white mushrooms thrust up abruptly from the clammy ground.

Putting his face flush with the carpet, he looks up, eyeing me.

Glowing faintly in the inky wood, mushroom heads thrust up.

And jumps to his feet.

Thrust up! Thrust up!

I work hard not to thrust up myself.

Nearby, a slightly moistened face stares vacuously at them.

I raise my hand and say quietly, "I have a theory, if I may interject." He comes forward and stands directly over me. There he remains, still as a statue. I say, dryly, "Remember, you can't sit on my lap." He shows not a flicker of emotion. I look up directly at him and say clearly and carefully, "For whatever reason, it frightens you that our relationship has become so important you actually dread the weekend and missing me. I suggest you are dealing with your own fear by frightening me. At this very moment you're standing over me like an assailant, carrying your cane like a weapon. This after announcing the gang, whose members carry on like trash-talking teenagers while you behave in an intimidating manner."

The statue backs off and says matter-of-factly,

My hometown Maebashi lies in the foothills of Mount Akagi. The houses here are low and excessively gloomy. When the snow thaws, buds burst open in the foothills, and yet day in and day out snow on the peak glitters dazzlingly white!

I nod my head repeatedly, mulling over his statement. I say, "Foothills bursting with spring buds, the peak glittering with snow—foothills and peaks inhabit different worlds. So do you and I. You are in a world of pain."

Blizzards eddy everywhere now, blizzards swirl up and dim every ward in my town. Blizzards swirl. Blizzards swirl up over huddled houses teeming with the dreary clamor of young children.

"Blizzards destroy the boundary between town and peak. Your behavior is like a blizzard, obscuring the fact you are frightened by the weekend break. Clamorously you want to shove that sharp pain into me."

Seedlings gleam into azure skies. A child scoops out the soil. After looking for unsprouted seeds, I yanked my pale fingers from the bottom of that cheerful flowerpot.

"And ran off with a lice-infested gang which talks dirty."
He once again prowls the room, giving off an air of arrogance and, by-and-by, palpable hate. He plops himself down on the floor, crosses his legs and stares at the carpet.

Although half-buried in sand, the clam's outstretched tongue licks vigorously. Gravel and sea water grate noisily over this mollusk's head.

Syllable by syllable, he explains,

This clam, you see, is extremely gaunt. Note how its flabby innards have begun to rot! This clam will definitely sit on the sallow seashore and breathe out flash after flash of putrid breath.

He takes his cane and begins twisting it in the palm of his left hand.

Buffing the silver tip of my slim cane, how I'd love to drive out every grief as easily as I peel off and toss my gloves into the air.

Which is exactly what he does, letting them lie where they land.

My solitary self howls for a friend. Hurry here, nameless friend. Let's be serene and joyful today, you and I, with nothing to fret about. Let's embrace each other tenderly.

He jumps to his feet, hollering out,

Far from Mother, from Father, from siblings, let's link orphaned hearts invisible to parents. Out of the lives of all humanity, let's talk exclusively about your life and mine—only about our own shabby, forlorn and secret lives.

He laughs hysterically, stabbing his cane on the carpet as he repeats,

Shabby! Forlorn! Secret!

He bends over at the waist and turns his head toward me. He speaks mockingly.

Ah, won't our words scatter drearily over our laps like autumn leaves? I have the physique of a feeble and sickly child.

"You also have a weapon. And are in a very disturbed state of mind." Astonishingly, he hears me. He straightens up.

Carefully he lays the cane down on the couch.

Ah, once I climbed to the top of a high hill. Eyes fixed on the steep incline, I climbed as full of aspirations as any nobody. Once at the top, this worm of a nobody shed wretched tears. Nature everywhere distresses me and provincial conventions of human relationships depress.

I say quietly, "I agree. Provincial conventions of human relationships like ours. You're here out of profound need and that depresses you." He sits down on the couch.

My perverse, my puzzling self, wretched as a crow.

He takes a deep breath. He is exhausted. When time runs out, he picks up his cane, gets his gloves where he had tossed them and shuffles out.

I collapse in my chair and bust out laughing. A weekend? No, no, The Weekend! Uncanny how powerfully, how inevitably, how forever and a day every conversational partner I've ever worked with experiences weekend breaks with immense pain. Like every other nobody, Sakutarô climbed The Good Breast.

After all, he is alive. Amazingly, he experiences this elementary sanity as the act of a worm. A deep mystery. Yes, but how about the work of that marvelous couple, Melanie and Wilfred? There's a pair. Yes indeed. Melanie hammered into our brains the phenomenon of Splitting—The Good Breast/The Bad Breast. And Bion made another giant leap forward by identifying The Bad Breast with The Missing. He recognized that The Missing is not experienced as something absent. It's something present and very bad!

"Sakutarô, my love, tell me how bad it is, how palpably and excruciatingly and penetratingly bad The Weekend is. 'Provincial conventions of human relationships.' Yes, that The Breast needs a life of its own, time of its own, tending of its own. It's only human, after all."

Try telling that to the anguished, terror-struck Sakutarô. "I'm just taking the weekend off, Sakutarô. What's more provincial than that?" Try telling that to the howling infant.

I find it simply wonderful that Sakutarô demonstrates with the insight of genius the workings of the primitive mind. Wonderful! Wonderful!

And scary!

NOTES FROM ABOVEGROUND

To my Ningyoshisha colleagues

Two poet friends joined Sakutarô to form the Ningyo-shisha, the Merman Poetry Association. They aimed to study the interconnections among music, poetry and religion.

Glowing faintly in the inky wood, mushroom heads thrust up

Not many plants more easily associate with the glans penis than mushrooms.

Although half-buried in sand, the clam's outstretched tongue licks vigorously

Clams are universal figures of the vulva, which dominates Sakutarô's dreams. He often transformed himself into the object of his desire, so Sakutarô may be projecting his spiritual corruption on the clam's innards.

My solitary self howls for a friend. Hurry here, nameless friend

Reference to a friend is a common poetic conceit. Basically, the poet refers only to his troubled and distanced self. Nevertheless, though he regarded himself a worthless worm, he thirsted for a bosom buddy with whom he could share his sexual secrets and hopes for fame. His cantankerous arrogance and perversely "puzzling self" not only drove off any potential friend but separated himself from his self.

Provincial conventions of human relationships depress

Local morality demanded slavish conformity; belonging-to-the-group required the sublimation of "selfish individualism." Sakutarô, by contrast, believed that only free and intensely personal relationships could be ethical. He felt unwavering animosity toward the polity-centered feudal values that dominated his "village."

My perverse, my puzzling self, wretched as a crow

Japanese designate crows and ravens as "messengers of death," so no one would welcome a crow into his home. This bird thus symbolizes Sakutarô's sense of being rejected and alienated. He was so enamored of the crow that he designed a stylized crow icon to decorate a subsequent collection of aphorisms. In later years he sketched this icon beside his signature. Moreover, the publishers elected to stamp this crow icon in gold on the front cover of each of the fifteen volumes of his official works. It is safe to say that Sakutarô sported the crow symbol as though it was the Medal of Honor.

Having wheedled the needed yen from his parents, Sakutarô edited and published his first collection, *Howling at the Moon*. He had five hundred copies printed in January 1917, but the sale date was delayed by censors who required the elision of two poems that allegedly "corrupted public morals." In January he also published "Putrid Clam," "My Solitary Self," "Sickened Seabed," and "Tender Affection"—all of which are dealt with in this book. On February 15, Sakutarô put three hundred copies up for sale. Most sold by the end of March. As he had predicted, *Howling at the Moon* created quite a stir among Tokyo poets and critics. Based on several baffled or astonished reactions, however, he had ample room to complain that because true art is difficult to grasp it wasn't surprising that so few could truly understand his work.

Session
Disgusting Scenes
20

Notes from Underground

Somewhat to my surprise, Sakutarô shows up for the next session, albeit late. He comes into the consultation room but remains standing in the middle of it. "The statue's back," I say to myself, but my flippancy suddenly gives way to fear.

Suppose the statue comes to life? At least it hasn't brought that damn cane. Sakutarô opens and clenches his hands with the regularity of a metronome, staring at a far corner. A look of nausea washes across his face. Reminds me of that extremely gaunt clam he mentioned last time, its flabby innards beginning to rot. How'd he put it? Breathing "out flash after flash of putrid breath."

It crosses my mind he's using his hands like the in-and-out breathing of that putrid clam. Just a guess, so I say nothing. I feel a wave of nausea. Amazing how humans can push into each other's innards. This vulnerability is precisely what Melanie proposed is the secret to human growth and development. Every mind structure comes into being by passing through another mind. Language is the most obvious example, but it's true in a much more vivid fashion in the projection of hugely powerful emotions. Melanie thought the capacity to take in another's suffering and confusions is the chief requirement for The Good Breast to do its civilizing work. Bion observed that the most horrifying experience for all of us is, "I am dying."

Sakutarô turns away, stopping my reflections. He mutters "Sickened Seabed" and lies down on the couch. He speaks rapidly.

Disgusting scenes: Starfish mouths. Fish ears. The hand of a turbo shell. The sea slug's scarlet camellia blooming in globs from a sea urchin's flaccidly festering flesh.

I'm scared, which is not a problem—if I can keep working. I remember Bion quoting a famous general who said, "You don't have to be very intelligent to be a general, but you must be able to use such brains as you have while being bombed and shot at." That helps.

Under the feeble light that a stringy medusa casts, a rheumatic octopus eats one of its tentacles, eats a blue clam.

"Reminds me of the shadows of dreadful monsters you once described on the walls of your mind."

The jam-packed shellfish in these shallows also feast on the raw roots of my nerves.

"Biology eats on you. So you attack the disgusting, living world. Sickened seabed. Festering flesh. An octopus eating one of its tentacles. 'Take that, biology! And that! And that!'"

With unmistakable and fathomless contempt, he spits out,

Oh, woman, I'm sure you'll chomp the grassy green with your firm, your comely teeth.

"I suggest you link a milk-producing cow with woman, presumably udders with breasts."

Oh, woman, I'll use the ink of this pale green grass to dye every inch of your face to quicken your craving. Then we'll indulge ourselves unobserved in this dense grass.

"A woman shares her biology with a cow—both produce milk—and both animals, if you will, participate in sexual life."

Mincingly in a falsetto he replies,

Look, here a bellflower nods its head and there a gentian gracefully ripples its fingers.

Sighing, oozing contempt, he goes on,

Ah, I hold you ever so tight as you urge me on with your every wile.

With the suddenness of finding a snake in one's path, he hisses,

Thus do we mate like snakes in this deserted field.

He's out the door before I can blink. Gone as silently and

instantaneously as a snake in the grass. Well, well, well! I understand better why Japanese censors nixed some of Sakutarô's work. One dimension of Sakutarô's genius is that he experiences at an all but unbearably high pitch humanity's grievous suffering unleashed by sexual conflicts. Little wonder the Church Fathers opted for celibacy back in the 12th century. Get around Sex altogether. Expunge biology—grass, shellfish, snakes, cows, woman. Alas, Sakutarô makes plain we're much more human and much more biologic than otherwise. East is east and West is west, but when it comes to Sex, the twain do meet. Sakutarô registers with the heightened sensibility of genius how tragically Sex and biology bring great suffering in uncanny fashion to the race. One thing's certain about Sakutarô—he's a card-carrying member of the species, *Homo sapiens sapiens*.

I keep only one book in my office, William Benzon's *Beethoven's Anvil*. Benzon's a neuro-cognitive scientist and a musician. I open his book for the umpteenth time. Benzon blows a mean trumpet, and he taps out a gorgeous riff on Melanie and Wilfred for me whenever my soul needs help. He introduced me to the work of William Condon who studied the rhythmic structure of human speech communication. No great ape gives any evidence of a sense of rhythm. Apes don't synchronize with one another and can't hold a steady beat.

Not so for hominids. Condon discovered a close synchrony between a speaker and a listener, what he described as "interactional synchrony." A listener's body movements lag about forty-two milliseconds behind the vocal patterns of the speaker, "like a car following a continuously rapidly curving road."

Once again I turn to *Anvil*, page twenty-six: "Infants exhibit near adult competence at interactional synchrony within twenty minutes of birth." Wouldn't Melanie have loved to know that back in 1946—here the neurologic underpinnings of projective identification identified. Benzon writes, "The ability to match one's movements to another's seems to be a condition of normal interaction with others. When this capacity is hampered, as it is in dyslexia and autism, communication is compromised. Synchrony creates a space of communicative interaction, a coupling between two brains in which each can affect the other's internal states." Oh yes, including experiencing someone else's nausea.

Benzon proposes that interactional synchrony started with music and dance. These rhythmic activities he condenses into a social principle: human beings create a uniquely human social space when their nervous systems are coupled through "interactional synchrony. "

Interactional synchrony is not conscious or deliberate. It is not something one thinks about; it just happens, at least for most of us. Interactional synchrony is working at birth, which implies it is mediated by core brain structures that are phylogenetically old, for only these structures are operative at birth. The newest and largest brain structure, the cerebral cortex, is an uninsulated mass of nerves incapable of coherent processing at birth. Its fibers become insulated over the first several years of life.

That is, tightly synchronized interaction with others constitutes part of the maturational environment for the cerebral cortex. The Good Breast creates human beings. Not biology. Not conjoining of egg and sperm. A conjoining of human mother and infant.

Notes from Aboveground

Oh, woman,
I'll use the ink of this pale green grass
to quicken your craving

These lines come from the poem "Tender Affection," one of two pieces Sakutarô was obliged to excise from the first edition of *Howling at the Moon*. Censors claimed that it "offended public morals." On the surface "Tender Affection" depicts an incidence of sexual intercourse on an open field, which was taboo. It made no difference to the censors that this extremely stylized and unreal description amounted to little more than wishful thinking. It's no doubt true, as Sakutarô claimed, that descriptions of lovemaking in Song of Solomon are far more realistic and therefore more "offensive to public morals" than anything in *Howling at the Moon*.

In what sense might green "quicken [the woman's] craving"? Standing between the blue of the heavens and the red of hell, green has long been linked to Mother Earth, not to mention spring, innocence, hope, growth and fertility. It is furthermore the color of expectation. The Romans saw green as feminine, and because they designated green as Aphrodite's color, they related it to love.

Thus do we mate like snakes
in this deserted field

Snakes' sinuous movements may imply erotic desires. The Garden of Eden story makes the serpent a metaphor of temptation. Snakes can symbolize the unconscious. They may as well suggest perpetual change and sameness because, though they regularly shed their skin, they remain the same snake. Shedding may personify a questioning mind.

Session
Can't Suck Life from Your Thumb
21

NOTES FROM UNDERGROUND

Sakutarô does not show up for our next session. Had I pushed the envelope beyond his capacity to tolerate? Always a possibility. Or had I fatally blundered, like losing my patience recently? Doubtful. Mostly the work is threatened by a loss of nerve. Bion thought courage indispensable. In both partners!

Edmund Burke observed, in effect, "Those who are not present are always wrong." Only when you try it! During our last conversation, I experienced waves of nausea from Sakutarô exhaling toxic fantasies. That enabled me to participate viscerally in his sense of putrid and festering innards. From his gut directly into mine. Such communicative powers provide an indispensable basis for human growth and development. We don't become human by sucking a magical potion out of our thumbs. We become human through the work and emotional powers of other humans. We arrive on the planet in bits and pieces, as it were, and we can only get put together within the insides of emotionally indispensable others.

That's what Klein discovered in 1946, when she first described projective identification. In fact, her work, continuing that of Freud and taken up by Bion, can be thought of as a recognition human beings need to be taken in, in ways never realized.

That's what Sakutarô and I are learning afresh. What makes The Missing Weekend so terrifying for him is precisely his awareness that he needs to be taken in. And if he isn't, he will emotionally die. That sounds exaggerated. It is not. It is a fact that without the other we do not survive as human beings.

His dependency on the sessions reveals his terrifying vulnerability. Despite no particular goodness or specialness in him, he needs to be taken into the emotional innards of another human being or he will evaporate into the ether. That profound truth is dreadfully distressing. No wonder he turns to the gang, hollers for an orphaned friend, skips sessions in order to chase nameless women.

Little wonder he is missing today.

NOTES FROM UNDERGROUND

When I open the door to the waiting room, it almost bumps Sakutarô who is standing directly in front of it. He comes in like a runner out of the blocks and lies down on the couch. Before I get to my chair, he says sharply,

Listen to me, frog!

"This frog's listening!" I say hastily, as I sit down.

I imagine you pallidly puffed up. At dusk in the driving rain, you're croaking: *gyo-gyo-gyo-gyo*.

He croaks mightily.

This evening fierce winds and rain batter the darkened earth. Heaving sighs of relief over chilly blades of grass, you're croaking: *gyo-gyo-gyo-gyo.*

"Isn't the frog calling out for a mate?"

Listen to me, frog!

"I'm listening." His annoyance gets my attention. I'm on the wrong track.

You are seldom far from my mind. Lantern in hand, I study the gloom of my yard. My frame of mind gaunt, I stare into the foliage of bushes wilted by the rain.

"I suggest I am seldom far from your mind. Even on weekends, as we heard recently. In fact, especially on weekends, when we're not together. I am seldom far from your mind even when you miss a session."

No response.

"Today, you dash in and insist I listen to you. You need something. You're hurting, chilled with gloom and in a gaunt frame of mind. I suggest at the moment—how shall I put it? At this very moment you're cured. The cure may not last longer than your appreciation of the flute, but that's beside the point."

No response. I remember Wilfred giving a talk on cure when he first moved to the States. Hundreds of analysts had piled into the conference hall to hear the great man. With British modesty and charm, Wilfred described working with a woman who screamed every time he opened his mouth. This went on for months. One day when he ventured a thought during a session with her, "I forget what," he confessed. "Probably I had offered some bloody nonsense." The woman didn't scream. Instead she asked, "What did you say, doctor?" Bion wondered out loud, "Is that a cure?" and sat down.

Sakutarô stirs. In a flat voice, he says,

To Elena from an outing. One day we had stretched out on this summit's stunning patch of grass. Raising our eyes and gazing toward the faraway foothills, we felt we were viewing an expansive seascape. As wind surfed the sky, I strolled aimlessly over the lush green hilltop, a pebble to my lips.

"Let me get this straight," I say puzzled. "You're with your love, Elena, in a stunning patch of mountain overlooking the sea. You wander away from her and find yourself with a pebble to your lips. You're kissing a pebble, not Elena? Is that right?"

Even now, my thoughts are of you.

His mood darkens, and his body stiffens.

I dread the countryside. I dread the dirt-poor droves of people who live in dreary abodes. Whenever I sit on a paddy edge, huge wave-like masses of soil cloud my mind. The reek of rotting loam tattoos my skin. Rural air is cheerless and choking. The countryside's coarse touch repels. The stench of rough-grained animal hides agonizes me.

"You wander from an idyllic mountain top down to a countryside where you get assaulted on all fronts—eyes, skin, lungs, nostrils, an orchestration of agony. Correct?"
He shrugs.

"How did you get down so fast?"

He opens both hands slowly, clearly perplexed. He's inviting my thoughts. Didn't he practically run to the couch? With relief I realize where I went wrong. He wants me to clean his head. He needs what Melanie called The Toilet Mother.

"I propose we change your frog into a crying infant, one who's not been diapered for a long time. The child feels utterly miserable, cold, wet, battered by stench and mess, a baby desperate for its mother."

He turns his head away and stares up at the ceiling. By-and-by he says as though adding an afterthought,

Dreaming of a butterfly. Large, weighty wings spread out in my room.

I wait. He turns his head and seems to sink into the couch.

The butterfly's small, ugly face, its long feelers, and those massively weighty wings spreading out like paper.

"For all your powers as a writer, spreading out wings of paper lovely as a butterfly's, you recognize a small and need-ful face reaching out its feelers."

I lay awake between white sheets, calmly trying to dredge up memories of my dream.

"You hope to calm yourself through writing, but it does-n't work. It doesn't take away your suffering and agony. In fact, it dredges up memories of your outing with Elena."

He breaks into sobs, sobs all too human, not the mighty croakings of a cold-blooded frog. He asks for a tissue, reaching back his hand without moving his head. He wipes his face.

I dreamed I was, bawling like a small child. In a grass clump behind that empty house the soul of this forlorn lad wept like a slimy toad.

He cries anew. I hand him another tissue. He pulls himself together.

I say, "How can a small, forlorn child receive care if no one's home? The house is empty. Cure originally meant care, and you weep knowing how much you are in need of care. That realization brings you today. When you turn away—missing a session—or as you do in your outing with Elena, it doesn't take very long to fall off the mountain and end up in agony."

On my palm I heap a bit of dirt in which I plant a seed. I now water the dirt with my white sprinkling can. A chill penetrates my palm as water burbles over the dirt.

"In the countryside, in which you fell, dirt was linked with dirt-poor people and rotting loam. A hopeless situation, without remedy. No one to clean up the mess. Here, dirt and water combine to give life. You feel once more life is opening up to you. It burbles over your palm, chilling it with excitement and renewal."

Ah, I fling open May's faraway windows and stretch my hand into the sunlight. If only the landscape invigorates me, my skin will fragrantly warm and the seed on my palm will breathe tenderly with life.

"Reparative offerings you tender life through your gift of writing."

I long for love. I long for a humble-hearted maiden to love me, her hands trembling on the high green treetop. Quivering always in that high place with tender feelings that implore my love.

"So what goes wrong?"

I'm always gadding through alleyways with the mind of the shabbiest beggar.

He drags himself off the couch. Sprinter in, halting beggar out. Yes and no. He's been cared for and cleaned up. Cured.

NOTES FROM ABOVEGROUND

Sakutarô informs a friend around the time he wrote these poems that he regards himself less a genuine bard than a "seeker of truth," perhaps even a "devil in search of God." Yes, Sakutarô confesses in his letter, he's full of contradictions, for he believes in God but loves Satan.

To Elena from an outing

Elena's health had become quite precarious by the time this poem appeared in January 1917. Consumption claimed her in May. Lacking effective treatment, tuberculosis in those days was almost always fatal. It was by far the leading cause of death among youthful Japanese. Nearly everyone in Japan knew someone who'd died of TB.

I dread the countryside

In those days, more than eighty percent of all Japanese were peasants. Some of Sakutarô's negative physical reactions to the countryside doubtless originate in his being allergic to the fertilizers or mulches used on the crops. Farmers were also heavy users of human manure.

I'm always gadding with the mind of the shabbiest beggar

Of course, he never dressed shabbily. He saw himself a panhandler because until the end of his life he begged money from his mother for books, booze, cigarettes and travel.

NOTES FROM UNDERGROUND

Sakutarô sits slumped in the waiting room chair when I bring him into the office. He begins flat as a pancake.

He wakens from the soil. He spades the soil. He who spades the soil stands on the soil.

Mumble. Mumble.

Cheerless. Cheerless. Yes, sharp sickles gleam.

"We're back in the countryside."

Barley drifts through hazy skies. Rows of peasants. Rows of seeds.

"Seed, time and harvest. Across numberless centuries. Peasants spading the soil to provide three square meals a day, three hundred and sixty-five days a year, for themselves and their families."

Cheerless. Cheerless. He who spades the soil weeps.

Sounding even flatter than a pancake, he mumbles,

Searching the open sea. Not a plant grows on this shore. What a desolate strand. Whenever I calmly watch the whitecaps like this, I see wave mounting wave and a pale evening moon that appears to hover over the swells.

"Older than the endless cycles of the plant kingdom are those of the inanimate world, pulsing on like waves mounting on waves, the round and round circling of the moon hovering forever over the swells."

Today I sense the far-off glow of the winter sea. My heart glistens with tears as I listen to the lonely roar of mammoth waves. Ah, a day when my depressions are endless. Yes, face the flow of these huge swells and toll the silver bell of yearning and solitude. Ah, toll it for my hurting flesh, my hurting heart.

He raises both arms, undulating his hands and fingers back and forth.

The ghosts of my ancestors drag their long tails past me.

"You're certainly dragging your tail today," I observe gently.

He twists and fusses, trying to get comfortable. He sits up

and swings his feet to the floor. He smiles at me. Nods and smiles again. I am completely nonplussed. I haven't the foggiest notion what's going on. Once more he turns to me, smiles sweetly, bows slightly and announces, like a grade school child about to recite,

Spring sentiments. Its tang makes me spellbound—like a French cigarette's aromatic tar.

Well, unusual. I'm about to say that when he smiles and nods at me. He pipes up in a falsetto,

Silver-tinted bird songs. The resounding flute. Plants that quiver. Rain-soaked air.

He appears to follow his words, watching their tinkling sounds tiptoe daintily out of the room. His face brightens as he waves them good-by, once more undulating the fingers of one hand. Then he begins to crouch down. He lowers his voice to a basso profundo and intones solemnly,

Wherever one also hears a woman's seductive sobs, spring seems to arrive with moist turgidity.

He looks at me menacingly, his face darkened and huge. He edges toward me on the couch and growls,

Once into spring, my soul sprouts mass upon mass of fungi. They make me think of worms wriggling through rotted tree stumps in dense forests deep in the hills: poisonous mushrooms, amanita and the scarlet death cup.

So Herbert Rosenfeld's personality is not the problem after all. Wasn't Sakutarô cured just the other day? Cleaned up? Open to life? Why am I getting plastered by these mud-balls—masses of fungi? amanita? scarlet death cups? My conversational partner and I have gone backwards, wandering somewhere behind Square One.

He pipes up again in that falsetto, nodding and smiling. He's starting to grate on me like fingernails on a blackboard.

Spring has come. Spring has come. The joy of spring's coming recalls the resounding flute that quickens every creature's life.

Right on cue, his face darkens. He crouches down, thrusting himself closer and growls,

Sprouting here and there: mass upon mass of fungi and poisonous mushrooms. Thriving in shady thickets: faintly glowing varieties of the scarlet death cup.

He thrusts his face closer to mine and stares unblinking at me. I feel a chill. His recitation of death and decay leaves me spooked. Violence crackles. My head's a muddle. I look away but without moving my head. I purse my lips and furrow my brow. I lift my eyes and say simply, "You're frightening me."

He blinks but keeps staring. It occurs to me to take an overview of the last sessions. Any port in a storm. "Let's see, some sessions back you found weekends, when we don't meet, troublesome. So you found yourself an orphaned friend, far from mother and father. You attributed your behavior to your perverse and puzzling self. Is that correct?"

He did not reply but stopped staring. I took this for permission to continue my historical survey, something I rarely do. "You missed the next—no, the next session you likened sexual intercourse to two snakes mating in the grass. The next session you missed. The one after that is when you described turning away from Elena at a picnic and ending up a mess in that dreary countryside. Today you tell us of your endless depressions. You observe that spring creates life, which I assume has something to do with sex, but this time you end up in a truly spooky place, with mass upon mass of fungi and poisonous mushrooms."

He gets up and walks out.

"Wilfred," I say aloud. "What's happening?"

What's happening is that Sakutarô is having thoughts but has no mind with which to think them. They're too powerful. Mind-blowing thoughts about sex, obviously. About needing—me, mother, father—about needing a good bath. Bion investigated what happens to thoughts when there's no mind to think them. He called them "unthinkable thoughts" or beta elements. Benzon noted that until the cerebral cortex gets sufficiently myelinated, a neurologic platform for the emergence of mind does not exist. Bion, following Klein, insisted this biologically determined myelinization must be simultaneously conjoined with the work of The Good Breast for a benign outcome.

I smile remembering how gorgeously Benzon states this, "tightly synchronized interaction with others constitutes part of the maturational environment for the cerebral cortex." The infant is endlessly overwhelmed by terrifying thoughts. He cannot "think" them. What he can do, if he's fortunate, is to shove them into The Good Breast which brings the violence down to scale. "There. There."

Inside the mother's mind the infant develops his own. There his experiences—beginning with feelings—get ensconced and provided a context. They find a home. Melanie noted that our original home is the mother's body, and the containing and detoxifying function of The Good Breast is the origin of the human mind. Didn't Bion stress that intolerable suffering denudes mind, unbuckling thought-things and spewing them in all directions?

And isn't that exactly what's happening with Sakutarô? Too much insight? With his thinking apparatus a wreck, what's he to do? Where's he going to get a hammer to pound things back to scale? Instead of thinking thoughts, Sakutarô spews them in all directions—like those words he waved out of the room—bald little billiard balls. No hooks. No attachments. Drifting into the ether. Aimless as Brownian motion. No way to fasten them together to tell a story. What is Sakutarô to make of mass upon mass of fungi and poisonous mushrooms in a spring supposedly quickening every creature's life?

When I leave my office at the end of the day, I'm still shaken. Later that night I wake up from a nightmare, something to do with mushrooms. I'm wide awake, so I get out of bed and go to the fridge. I sit down at the kitchen table and nurse a glass of orange juice. "Scarlet death cup" echoes in my mind. So it's him who wrecked my night! I chuckle at Hagiwara's preciseness. "Scarlet death cup," I imagine him announcing. "Also known as an infant's experience of its belly while howling." Freud said it all begins with the unpleasure principle. Get rid of the pain.

I take a sip of juice. Why the nightmare, I wonder. Somewhat in schoolboy fashion I remind myself a dream is merely a container. Holds unpleasant thoughts so we can sleep. That simple. Freud always started with biology. What is more fundamental than regulating sleeping and waking? I couldn't build a dream container strong enough and disguised enough to get me through the night.

I knew Sakutarô would be a handful, so no big deal. Maybe God is warning me in a dream! That chill this afternoon comes back. I blame it on the orange juice. I replay in my mind's eye his waving good-by to his words as they daintily tiptoed out of the room. That was spookier than the poisonous mushrooms and fungi. So, he's lost it, his mind. No wonder he spooked me. I have a nightmare to prove it.

His "endless depressions" turned into a fungus-like mass of unthinkable thoughts, erupting like poisonous mushrooms. How much pain can he put up with? What was that crazy falsetto stuff? Like scratchings on a blackboard, that's what. Made no sense to me. Dream thoughts are supposed to not make sense. Please do not disturb. Animal sleeping. Freud figured out a dream is merely an apparatus to deal with thoughts too unpleasant to think about. Disguise those unthinkable thoughts with a few tricks and stuff them in a dream. Good night and sleep tight. Not tonight.

I experience a moment of enlightenment (It's three o'clock in the morning so I remind myself that this may parse differently in daylight). A thought-thing is a sense experience, a feeling. Often terrifying. Feelings and the fantasies associated with them—Bion's beta elements—are fueled by instinctual energies and register as extremely powerful. The task is to make these thought-things thinkable. You can't think about an agglomeration—mud balls, like masses of fungi—plastering you in the face. Alpha-function, a term also made up by Bion, puts this unthinkable mess in order. Alpha function takes a beta element like terror and gives it a name like poisonous mushrooms, amanita, scarlet death cups. It transforms the feeling-fantasy into alpha elements. These are discrete, with hooks and a console of bells and whistles. One can link them into patterns. An unthinkable thought-thing becomes thinkable.

Like mother's work, alpha-function is never done. At least if you undertake ZamaZama, as Sakutarô has chosen. Freud's very first analytic patient, Frau Emmy von N., expressed horror at her unthinkable thoughts. "How dreadful it would be if they were to come to life!" Under conditions of Scientific Conversation that's precisely what happens, and it's hell to pay. That's why I'm awake at this cruel hour. And Sakutarô stormed out of the session today, overwhelmed by experiences too horrible to contemplate. Like Hamlet's Ghost, "O horrible! O horrible! Most horrible."

None the less, Sakutarô, for reasons unknown, chooses to undertake this journey into his interior. That's what makes him write. He risks bringing to life these unthinkable thought-things because he wants to make them thinkable. Scientific Conversation, as invented by Freud, does not have exclusive rights to this enterprise. There are many venues in the franchise. The most common product of alpha-function is words, but so are musicians' notes and painters' pigments. Any alpha element can be used to make unthinkable thought-things thinkable. Once thinkable, they can be used to tell a story, weave a narrative, discover patterns. Poets use alpha elements when they build out of airy nothingness—powerful beta elements—a local habitation and a name. In today's conversation, Sakutarô's thinking apparatus was a wreck, spewing his thoughts in all directions. Serves him right. He considers himself a "seeker of truth," perhaps even a "devil in search of God." He's asking for it. The horror is what he gets for being one of those rare creatures who decides thinking through "the darker aspects of the psyche" is preferable to getting pushed around thoughtlessly by them.

From the perspective of psychoanalysis, he is a god-like creature with infinite powers of language trying to make the devil merely an aspect of the human world.

Notes from Aboveground

In April 1917 Sakutarô contended that the spiritual sound-ness of his friend and fellow poet, Murô Saisei, resembled Tolstoy's wholeness. By contrast, Sakutarô thought that—in his intense concern for the darker aspects of the psyche—he closely resembled Dostoyevsky. Interestingly, he believed that his tone was not despairing but hopeful. He claimed, too, that he liked to write in the heat of inspiration, trying only to harness the intuitions and insights flowing through his mind. More often than not he himself couldn't grasp what he'd written until some months later.

He wakens from the soil. He spades the soil

The first sentence contains a resonance with the Genesis creation myth that describes Yahweh creating Adam out of the dust—or the slime—of the earth. In a sense, then, the Earth is thus mankind's mother. The figure of a spade, a phallic symbol, digging into the soil implies penetration. Obviously anyone who spades the soil controls it.

The ghosts of my ancestors drag their long tails past me

"Long tails" suggest the vaguely delineated lower-half of insubstantial and sexless specters or ghosts. The term "ancestor" invariably connects with fate and genes—very convenient "scapegoats" that absolved Sakutarô of the need to be responsible for his acts.

Hagiwara Sakutarô, 1924

PART III

Emergence of
Thinking Apparatus

NOTES FROM UNDERGROUND

Sakutarô shows up on time and appears in fine fettle. Until this moment I forget feeling spooked at the last session. Even forget my nightmare. I'm pleased at my forgetfulness. Bion made a point of having no memory and no desire when entering afresh into a conversation—no remembrance of a previous session and certainly no hopes for any particular outcome. It's always the first day of creation. Of course I violated this dictum when I provided that historical survey of sessions past. The sadness in Sakutarô's voice surprises me.

Where find the beds in which our dejected hearts can find repose? Are there feather beds where we can curl up between white quilts? Without such beds, we men have endlessly joyless hearts.

"We men?"

All the girls have beds. All girls have slender simian limbs; they snuggle together like songbirds in their huge white beds. All the girls sob with joy in those beds.

"I will restate what I hear you saying in terms of Freud's Two Principles of Mental Functioning—the girls luxuriate in the Pleasure Principle, while the men get stuck with the Reality Principle."

We, too, long to melt into tears. But in the hunt for humanity's spacious beds, our male hearts are destitute and charged forever with grief—hunting those beds where hearts melt utterly into one as though snuggling up in deep snow—hunting those beds of boundlessly beautiful love.

"You sound like Adam cast out of paradise forever wandering through the piled-up centuries, hunting those lost beds of boundlessly beautiful love. Little wonder your male heart is destitute and charged with grief."

He gives an involuntary twist and shakes his head as though physically warding off what I just said. He replies as flatly as an accountant reeling off numbers,

It's good to love this lovely city. It's good to love the structures in this lovely city. It's good to visit this city and prowl its lively thoroughfares where I can pursue its every tender-hearted girl.

"You tell us men are not allowed to have feelings and..."
He interrupts and tosses off,

Don't countless sparrows also love to twitter in the cherry trees that line these metropolitan avenues?

"I suggest what I'm drawing to your attention is no more than the twittering of a sparrow."

He mumbles something about the phantom of a blue cat, and then I hear,

I figure I'll track whatever phantoms exist and pine for Tokyo even on days when it sleets. That man-like beggar leaning chilled against an alley wall—what dreams does he dream?

"Oh," I respond, with a casualness matching his, "he probably dreams of boundless beautiful love and beds where hearts melt utterly into one and lucky are the girls who get all the breaks and curl up in feather beds between white quilts. Anyone you know?"

The next instant he leaps off the couch and jumps into my face, ending an inch from me. He screams something like:

Why did you say that?

I am terrified. My entire chest and abdomen feel completely emptied except for a tiny beating heart. I say, "Because I thought it was true."

He lies back down on the couch. I feel a wave of immense rage. Sakutarô just gave me the biggest scare of my life. He lies silent, for which I am grateful. I collect myself, reassembling my insides organ by organ. I remember Bion warning if one actually tries to do psychoanalysis in a real consultation room, there's a chance of being able to say, "That is what I call envy!"

I try desperately to get my thinking tools in some semblance of working order. I wrestle with my rage. Bion maintained that violent projective identification could make him feel persecuted as if someone in fact had banged dreadful feelings into him.

I see Sakutarô's face banging into me. That's a beta element! Not sprouting from remote poisonous mushrooms or even masses of fungi. That was as real as my emptied interior. An unthinkable terrifying flying missile, that's what it was. I remember my response and a hint of gratitude comes. I hadn't shattered completely. Nor had he. He did lie back down and, in fact, is right here in front of me. There's work to be done. Take a deep breath and get on with it. You did fine. You both survived. No irreversibility, that most dreaded of outcomes.

Dread constantly makes my honed sensibilities tremble like wind-jostled reeds.

"I understand your dread, as I'm still trembling like a wind-jostled reed. I can say with utmost conviction that what you experience is dreadful."

To my amazement, he starts to cry. My head has cleared, but I feel completely drained.

Woman! Hold me tight with your lovely, dauntless right arm and tenderly, so tenderly, calm my trembling afflicted heart.

"While you're at it, woman, and I'm not being in any way facetious, do the same for me."

Just hold me tight, and as you caress my shoulder place your dear warm hand over my fragile heart. Ah, put your hand here on my heart, woman, then speak to me with your tender, tear-tinged words: "There, there now, don't be afraid, don't you fear a thing. Always snuggle close to me,

to my robust heart, to these beautiful hands, to these arms, to this chest."

Tears flowing copiously down his face, he adds oh so softly,

"To these dauntless breasts."

He spends the remaining minutes weeping. When time expires, I say, "We'll have to stop here." He gets up, feverishly wiping his face with his hands. I offer him a tissue, which he takes. He pauses long enough to wipe his tears and leaves.

"Omigod!" I say out loud. I am glad to be alive. I think of Galileo, the Inquisition shoving its monolithic jaw into his face, screaming, "Why did you say that!" All the while rattling instruments of torture. It's really hard not to be a big scaredy cat—if you get tested.

I've sweated through my shirt. That somehow comforts me. I'm also freshly puzzled. What is his dread about? What hurled him off the couch? Surely not that stuff about the Pleasure Principle and Reality Principle. Sounds silly now I ever brought that bookish stuff up. What's blowing his mind, overwhelming his mental apparatus?

Some dreadful thought has been banging around for some time now. The scarlet death cup. The missed session. The dreadful countryside. Beta elements as gentle as those words daintily exiting the room, or as messy as those mudballs of fungi or as absolutely terrifying as his screaming an inch from my face. What are we missing?

I have no idea. It's not that girls have it made and boys don't. It has to do with murder. What else? I'm glad to be thinking again.

Notes from Aboveground

Beds in which our dejected hearts can find repose

Japanese conventions against men openly expressing their feelings the way women do are far more powerful than those in the West. Sakutarô envied women's "social permission" to indulge and display emotions. Japanese men who wish to expose their feelings turn to poetry. In 1917 when "Seeking Beds" appeared, few Japanese slept in a Western-style bed, especially a feather bed. Sakutarô was that rare exception. He insisted on wearing pajamas and used a cot at least from 1914 to 1919, when he married.

It's good to love this lovely city

The "lovely city" is Tokyo. The "blue" of "Blue Cat" captures the English sense of being forlorn or melancholic. The poet, a sad tomcat, sets out at dusk to hunt for romance or oblivion. This work graphically depicts the image of an alienated modern urban man; it is one of Sakutarô's most famous, most anthologized, and most often cited poems.

Place your dear warm hand over my fragile heart

Since childhood, Sakutarô's health had never been robust. Nor did heavy drinking and smoking help. Above all else, he remains a poet of his own intimate interiors and confidences. He attempts to penetrate the psyche rather than merely to probe nature. The poet's anguish establishes itself as a kind of "static presence" in the mind. It refuses to go away.

Session
Murdered, Drawn
and Quartered

NOTES FROM UNDERGROUND

Sakutarô comes in looking exhausted and drained. He hasn't shaved, his hair's uncombed, his clothes look as if he's slept in them. He speaks in a low voice. I have to lean forward in my chair to hear him.

The girl's color was white. Her color emanating from the snow sparkled marvelously from head to toe.

He mumbles something.
"I didn't hear what you said."

Depressing riverbank...,

he replies with a burst of annoyance. Silence. By-and-by,

I close my eyes and try chomping into a plant root so I can

suck its sap the way I suck depression's bitter juices. In truth, I have no hope that doing so will help, for my life is but one incomprehensible depression after another.

"I suggest what is incomprehensible is not your depression. The mystery is that you chomp on a plant root and suck its bitter juices. Depression will follow predictably such a remedy, wouldn't you say?"
He retorts with weary exasperation,

Well, it is the rainy season, time for clammy, drizzling rain. However you think of it, yes, it's rain! rain! and more rain!

"Ah, it's the weather. Now, why couldn't I figure that out!"

Wondrous herbaceous plants flourish here, not to mention various pathetic winged bugs skittering along the shore, skittering around morosely.

"Lousy weather and now these damn bugs." My sassiness brings to mind his screaming in my face. I don't care. I feel secure, not reckless. The game is on. In a twinkling everything changes. It's uncanny. I have witnessed this a thousand times. Sakutarô heaves a deep sigh and says with measureless grief,

This heart of mine always played quietly by itself. Ever since my long-past boyhood, this cheerless heart has cast a shadow over my path through life. The shadow of solitude deepens little by little, and the glooms of my dreadful depressions surge.

I experience deep sadness. I've grown fond of Sakutarô.

On the verge of tears, I sense Melanie taking my hand. It was she who discovered that miraculous shift from what she called the paranoid-schizoid position to the depressive one. It happens like a conversion, "in a moment, in the twinkling of an eye." Sakutarô has caught a giant wing that sweeps the two of us into a rapturous turbulence where larks sing at heaven's gate. The shift to the depressive position soars on a dawning realization that the difficulties and griefs one experiences are of one's own doing. "I'm the problem."

The good news is that I can do something about "me." Dreadfully depressing to discover one is so prone to act mean-spirited and ornery and contrary, but one senses this discovery as truth and only that can lead to growth and mastery.

I'm sitting alone now in my room where I gaze into the darkness of my sinking soul. Impotent as a resting fly, my soul sighs wretchedly. My life meanders ineffectively through spring's quietly setting sun.

He stops and covers his face with his hands. Interrupted by sobs he whispers,

As I rest fly-like on a windowpane, my life listens to the sobbing song of a forlorn child.

"Also a contrary child," I add gently. "A child who does not press its mouth against the breast but turns to bitter roots. You've struggled against this contrariety as long as you can remember. It has cast its cheerless shadow over your entire life. There's comfort here—your inconsolable grief is not incomprehensible but condign."

Silence. Time passing. I remember Freud's very first "analytic" patient, Frau Emmy von N. She too experienced one marvelous moment, recognizing herself as the problem. Freud pointed out to her that from that perspective her sufferings were condign. That's where that word came from! I also reflect that Frau Emmy turned from that brief moment in the light and plunged into bottomless perdition, estranged from everyone, imprisoned forever with madness.

I sense the monster gathering itself again on the couch and beginning to tower over us. From the depressive state back to a paranoid-schizoid one. No matter how thoughtful, sympathetic, attentive, gentle, mellifluous, unwavering, brilliant one may be, back and forth it goes—if the conversational partner is fortunate and has the wherewithal to continue the brutal work. Frau Emmy tolerated only one moment of sanity before disappearing into The Shades, never to be heard from again.

Flicking his wrist daintily, Sakutarô breaks his silence.

White butterflies dart everywhere. Ah, their honed little wings glittering, glittering, glittering, glittering, glittering among thick gaps in the foliage. They flit about in prodigious swarms—*teh-foo, teh-foo, teh-foo, teh-foo, teh-foo, teh-foo, teh-foo.*

He breaks off his derisive sing-song. In a deep growl, dripping contempt, he bellows,

Yes, what a depressing delusion! These weighty limbs, weighty hearts, gloomy knots of matter heaped endlessly on matter. Yes, what beautiful aberrations. I see in this wood both women's weighty, cast-off limbs and the bewitching ponderousness of dissipated thighs and breasts.

There it is—the unthinkable thought that's been banging around the last weeks. Murder of woman. Followed by dismemberment! No wonder he screamed in my face. He's in a nightmare world but wide awake. How do you wake someone up when they're already awake? The nightmare he shoved me into presented a trivial problem. All I had to do was wake up and drink some orange juice. Sakutarô has plunged into the deepest region of the primitive mental apparatus, the fantasy of hacking The Good Breast to bits out of envy and frustration. Navigating this nether region is where courage comes in; necessary but not sufficient. What one has to elaborate, on the spot, by articulating alpha elements—or whatever you want to call them—is a mind that can contain and think the unthinkable. Or the whole enterprise blows sky-high.

"I have a theory," I say calmly and dryly. "As I've pointed out many times, my theories are a dime a dozen. Only you're able to provide the data that supports or refutes a theory." I pause and clear my throat. In fact, I am clearing a space for thinking out of our conversational "tissue" that correlates with mind space. The pace of my speech, its phonological contour, its syntactical preciseness, are physical realities for Sakutarô to grab hold of and protect himself from the relentless beta elements blasting him. My words register first as physical objects, available to cohere like the layers of a shield. At the same time, I must make evident a sense of security.

Flippancy is fatal, whistling in the dark a disaster, cluck-clucking likewise. And I must keep clear with Sakutarô the fact of his Isolation without abandoning him. The horror is his doing, its management his responsibility. I'm not authorized to deal with this huge task, trotting out some prescriptive nostrums. Or assuring him I've been where he is. He's him. Unrepeatable. Wandering in regions unique to his self. I haven't been where he is. Sure, we're much more human than otherwise. But Sakutarô has to pay the piper for being Sakutarô. I list a number of beta elements that have whizzed around. Slowly. Dryly.

"You've mentioned many items recently that puzzled me: Poisonous mushrooms. A French cigarette's aromatic tar. Stench of animal hides. Rotting loam. Slimy toads. Amanita. Worms wriggling through rotted tree stumps. At our last session you leaped off the couch. My theory is that what you're glimpsing you just now called beautiful aberrations. If we change beautiful to dreadful, a word you frequently make use of, then I suggest all these odds and ends and bits and pieces begin to cohere and make sense."

He sits up but slowly, so I am not frightened. He clutches his head with both hands and stares straight ahead.

Ghosts from Macbeth drift before me. My heart's pounding. He's about to send a dispatch from a region of unfathomable darkness.

Here and there lips heap up suffocatingly like fresh blood. They jam together on the bloodless lips of my corpse, on my forehead, on my head, on my hair, on my crotch, on my thighs, on my armpits, on my ankles, my soles, on both my right and my left arms, and on my belly, too.

Once more, slowly and dryly, I respond. "I have another theory. I think you're cured. You have transformed unconnected but dreadful items like poisonous mushrooms and wriggling worms into recognizable items that can be accurately named and put together into a story. It's not a happy story, certainly, but it's one that yields meaning. You fantasize tearing a woman to pieces with your teeth and lips. That's precisely what Melanie Klein discovered in her work with children. Out of rivalry and envy and frustration and disappointment with the mother, a child experiences unmanageable rage and murderous feelings. That's scary, to put it mildly. However, if one can tell a story, no matter how wild the details, one can think about one's experience and tell it to others. We're not getting suffocated by the blood and gore. We're putting them into a story, here in broad daylight."

Obscene clumps of matter swarm together in masses.

"Can't put clumps into a story. They're just a scary mass. I can understand murderous envy, which is what you're struggling with, because Melanie told me the same story you're telling. Same character. Different name. Envy spoils. If I can't have The Breast for myself, I will rip it apart and spit it out so no one else can have it either."

Yes, these so excessively and dreadfully depressing, these unbearable and agonizing pulsations of sex.

A thought troubles me. Is Sakutarô heading for a Major Depressive Disorder? That's a brain problem, not a mind problem. It gets kindled by overwhelming distress. What do I do then? No anti-depressants are available. Won't be for thirty years. Tofranil, the first anti-depressant, appeared on the scene in the late 1950s. Sakutarô and I are working sometime in the 1920s. Now what? I have misgivings we ever started this journey. Sow the wind and reap the whirlwind.

No, I remind myself. Isolation. Sakutarô's the one responsible. I never told him to start this conversation. Or to unravel the workings of his mind. No more than anyone told Freud to undertake self-analysis. It's Sakutarô's decision. His the risk. His to pay for disturbing, like Freud, the sleep of the world.

Sakutarô reels off the couch and out of the room.

What sense could I make of all this without Freud and Melanie and Wilfred? Some folks have all the luck. Like me.

Notes from Aboveground

Well, it is the rainy season, time for clammy, drizzling rain

The rainy season deprived Sakutarô of the will to do anything and afflicted him with ennui. He felt only like lying on a sofa—a clearly exotic reference because few homes then had sofas—and gazing out the window at the rain. Baudelaire described ennui as the state of those aware the world had invaded them; they hypocritically refuse, however, to admit they've been violated. Sakutarô knew.

Apathy, boredom and inertia so demoralized him that he began reading Western philosophy—Bergson, James, Kant, Nietzsche, Plato, Schopenhauer. He concluded that most writers offered little more than theories and abstract "solutions." No help. Worse, these pseudo-solutions merely intensified his ennui and increased his skepticism. In the end, he doubted he'd ever discover satisfactory answers— till in Los Angeles he ran into Freud, Klein and Bion. Posthumously.

I'm sitting alone now in my room
where I gaze into the darkness of my sinking soul

Sakutarô once claimed he wrote verse as a "protest of my solitude." This poem, "Fly Songs," significantly begins by implying the closeness of spring when hormones drive the poet up the wall—or the window. The fly conjures images of impurity and filth, for this insect taints the innocent. One of Beelzebub's appellations is "Lord of the Flies."

Session 26

Mind Arrows into the Conversation

Notes from Underground

Sakutarô has changed astonishingly. Flushed, he strides jauntily into the office, sporting newly-pressed clothes.

Before lying on the couch, he sings out,

My bursting emotions resemble buds of life that burgeon as steadily as a tall tree arrowing into the sky. Reaching high, chest extended, the tree seems able to touch the blue merely by stretching. My feelings inhale spring's exceedingly glorious air the way songbirds feed, delighted to open their mouths.

He smiles happily at me. He lies down and hurries on.

Oh, how appealing the continuous burgeoning of life's buds! Oh, how steadily both herbaceous and woody plants reach up together!

"I suggest you're delighted we make such a good pair. Sturdy like wood. Burgeoning like buds. We both show up today standing tall and ready to carry on. Our steadiness reassures you."

A smile lights up his face. He waves his left hand, holding it above him. He turns it this way and that, inspecting it.

What about the hand's genuine allure and amplitude? What about its confection-like plumpness? Its fingers, too, are truly dainty and elegant, quite like pale little fish—their gently fluttering movements irrepressible.

"It sounds to me you're describing a woman's hand, not yours."

He laughs, throwing his left hand away and bringing his right hand to his lips.

Oh, I want to kiss her hand. I want to take it whole into my mouth and feed on it.

Waving "her" hand and breathing in its scent deeply, he asks,

What about those tastefully fabulous flowers blooming in the hollows between her fingers? Those hollows exude musk-like aromas reminiscent of dew-sprinkled peach blossoms. Ah, I cherish every single, smoothly buffed finger, wanting to wrap my lips around it and endlessly suckle it. Ah, these cravings—as impertinent and as testily contrary as a child's.

"Hmmm," I offer. "I have a very different theory from yours. Of course you have the last word. I suggest your cravings are wonderfully pertinent and anything but contrary.

The centerpiece of your creativity as a writer is your hand, even as the breast is of the mother. When you toss aside your hand, you allow a place for hers, acknowledging its genuine allure and amplitude. You form a partnership with her as intimate and interlocking as that of herbaceous and woody plants reaching up together.

"You don't bite the hand. You kiss it. You wrap your lips around it and endlessly suckle it. Her hand brings to mind the delicate beauty of a dew-sprinkled peach blossom, and you sing of its inexhaustible abundance, its participation in the continuing flow of life."

The flush vanishes. I am taken aback. What's happening? He knits his brow, abruptly deep in thought. When he next speaks, he is accessing an entirely different region of his mind.

Flourishing on the grounds of that vacant house: pines, loquats, peach trees, black pines, sasanquas, cherry trees. Plants under dense foliage, moreover, grow awesomely lush, rank with the likes of ferns, bracken, osmunds, and dewgrass—a jumbled mass carpeting the ground.

"You have generated alpha elements from your relationship with The Breast/Hand, and these articulating elements enable you to take thought. How? You name things. Like Adam named the animals. Before you can tell me what you're thinking, I have to know what it is you're thinking about. Ah, now I know—pines, loquats, peach trees, ferns and bracken, and osmunds."

Night then radiates blanched beams of moonlight over this hushed realm. Coming into view under the moonlight are ferns, bracken, pine branches, and such, as well as the eerie activities of slugs, snakes, lizards, and their ilk. Ah,

my deeply pregnant, solitary yearnings for those never-solved enigmas, for the yard secrets of this vacant house seen so clearly in my dreams!

"Hear how names multiply! Perhaps the enigmas can never be solved, but you can name them now with the vocabulary you've created. Seeing the real world even under moonlight is far better than seeing things clearly in dreams. Freud discovered the only useful work dreams do is to keep us sleeping. That won't solve the secrets of nature."

Again he laughs. The second time today.

I'm a snake charmer,

he says charmingly.

I have the snake slither slowly from a woman's snow-white nape toward her swelling breasts. As the snake moves gradually downward, ah, it stealthily pales.

"What you're telling us is remarkable. As the snake moves gradually downward toward the swelling breasts, it changes color, becoming paled by the woman's snow-white nape. It is visibly changed by its relationship with the woman."

He shouts out,

Someone with a blanched mind is observing!

"Yes. Yes! The conjunction of the breast and the snake has created mind. Blanching indicates throwing light on something, an activity of mind. Mind observes. The blanched beams of the moonlight enable you to identify the plants and animals. It happened just a moment ago as you were talking. Under the radiance of The Good Breast, her hand in your metaphor, you found yourself with a vocabulary. You started to think. I will put it this way. The Good Breast vitalizes, the snake charmer structures. She sings. He names. You stated this metaphorically any number of ways today, such as the herbaceous and the woody plants reaching together. Or in human terms, hands clasped together."

A warm and fluffy bed adorned with lovely velvet. Yes, the bed I pine for, thirst after, and constantly dream of. The only bed I've ever sought.

"When not overcome by rivalry and envy of The Breast."

I would be toasty warm sleeping on that bed, for its velvet arms would embrace me. I'd bury my weary body in those huge breasts filled with life's every bliss.

"The fecundity of nature, pressed down and flowing over."

Ah, what joy to sleep for the first time on such a bed!

Our conversation rocks in gentle antiphon. After the session ends, I luxuriate in our work together. Until that worry returns—is he becoming brain ill, with manic defenses staving off a collapse into major depression? Melanie wrote a great deal about this manifestation of Denial. Is his good cheer an attempt to fly above those bad places we had toured recently, barely surviving? Gerard Manly Hopkins thunders into my mind. "But ah, but O thou terrible, why wouldst thou rude on me / Thy wring-world right foot rock? Lay a lion limb against me, / Me heaped there, me frantic to avoid thee and flee."

Get rid of the pain. Avoid and flee. ZamaZama's like the Lord: it giveth, it taketh away. Forget it, I tell myself. No memory. No desire. Sakutarô's next session will be the first day of creation.

Notes from Aboveground

What about the hand's genuine allure and amplitude

These lines derive from the poem, "Her Hand a Confection." Sakutarô was fond enough of this piece to include it in three collections. The kimono encourages a focus on the hands and the neck, which Sakutarô considered a woman's most sensuous parts. For him, being without sex constituted physical and psychic punishment.

Oh, I want to kiss her hand.
I want to take it whole into my mouth and feed on it

Critics claim that Sakutarô describes only the objective beauty of the female hand! Given his temperament, the imagery here could imply a desire for fellatio. In any event, he appreciated life mainly through intimacy with a woman.

What about those flowers blooming in the hollows
between her fingers

In the first version of this work, "hollows" was "crotch."

Those hollows exude musk-like aromas
reminiscent of dew-sprinkled peach blossoms

The Japanese word for "peach," a homonym for "thigh," has latent sensuous overtones.

Flourishing on the grounds
pines, loquats, peach trees
black pines, sasanquas

By carefully cataloging the plants and animals in the yard, Sakutarô engages in a degree of specificity that is quite foreign to the content of the average dream. Could this imply that poets see and dream far more attentively and concretely than the rest of us? Despite such powers, not even an artist can penetrate "the secret lives of these plants." Sakutarô thought that scientists had yet to clarify the most crucial and puzzling mysteries of human existence.

I have the snake slither from a woman's snow-white nape toward her swelling breasts

The woman wears a kimono, which means no brassiere stands in the snake's way.

Following the February 1917 publication of *Howling at the Moon*, Sakutarô moved from what he called the "psychic terror" of his first book to the hormone-driven, melancholic longings that characterize his second, *Blue Cat* (January 1923). He was keenly aware of the need to take a fresh look at all the familiar conventions, which insisted that poetry should uplift—and certainly avoid dealing with sexuality and personal problems.

Session

Eating from the
Tree of Knowledge

NOTES FROM UNDERGROUND

Sakutarô looks hung over. His alternating appearance from session to session provides a visual antiphony—one session he's decked out neat as a pin, the next he's a wasted drunk.

My feet stroll drunkenly through town. Drunken legs bereft of everything gad about Tokyo in search of its every illusive joy.

"Apparently it's your turn to get hacked to pieces, feet and legs severed. Legs run your life, gadding about aimlessly and mindlessly on their own, dragging you wherever."

Yes, hopeless legs collapse continuously on the street.

"Aren't you describing falling-down-drunk?"

My spent mind sleeps deeply through the night. What's that? A suckling child stirs serenely through my dream. I lament the bleached-out light in this room. Life's insipid throb makes me feel forlorn.

"Aren't you now describing a throbbing hangover?"
He shakes his head like a dog shaking off water.

Her milky, long, and always richly moistened nape recalls a fish swimming upstream from a deep dale. Imagine a fish swimming down her kimono collar!

He gives a low chuckle, more like a lurid grunt. Silence. And then a light goes on in my head.

"Let me tell you a story," I say brightly. "Stories make for easy listening, a kindness today, wouldn't you say?"

Silence. Fair enough.

"The story, of course, is about you. Everything we say here is about you. It's also a story you already know, and it goes like this. When God created a garden eastward of Eden for Adam, He gave him the run of the place except for one patch declared off-limits—The Tree of Knowledge. If Adam ate of that tree, he would surely die. Meanwhile, God gave Adam work to do, naming the plants and animals, exactly as you did the other day when you itemized loquats and sasanquas and bracken and osmunds—some of which I had never heard of. God also gave Adam a woman. One day, along came a serpent and slithered over to Eve, a coupling which empowered her to eat of that Tree of Knowledge."

Sakutarô gives a start, as though something just hit him on the head.

"Like your snake slithering slowly down the woman's nape, toward her swelling breast, the coupling of Eve with the snake produced a blanched and observing mind, creating knowledge. Having eaten of the Tree of Knowledge, Eve and Adam became aware of their nakedness. Knowledge of sex began the long story of human growth and development."

Sakutarô lies completely still, all ears. The game is on. "I worked with a mentor named Wilfred Bion. I have mentioned him before. He observed that naming something gives it a handle. I don't know what sasanquas and osmunds are, but I can hold a sasanqua or osmund by its handle before I even know what it is. Wilfred called the naming process alpha-function, its activity producing alpha elements, such as creating a biologic nomenclature. By the act of naming, Adam sorted the clumped mass of nature into discrete alpha elements, each clearly identified as a word in the dictionary.

"This made possible the next task, which was to come up with an apparatus that strings alpha elements together. Alpha elements, like words for example, have hooks or handles, coupling devices that allow the mind to tie them together into endless shapes and patterns. A nice example is weaving them into a story, as we're doing this very moment.

"This coupling apparatus Bion called Mind, and it behaves exactly opposite from your feet and legs today, which gave the boot to all other elements in your personality, kicking them out of your story. Your legs propelled you into drunkenness, one well-known way of destroying alpha-function."

Sakutarô's still all ears.

"Now, my mentor had a mentor in turn by the name of Melanie Klein. I've mentioned her before, too. Klein discovered a child fantasizes a penis in the breast, a primitive notion about the relationship between father and mother. Odd as that sounds, it is not surprising. The child assumes the breast is the center of the universe, that followed in turn by the centrality of the father's maleness. Suppose we think of the act of that breast swelling as the first step in alpha-function. It generates the vitalizing energy to name things, no easy task, and these names we'll label alpha elements. Then, when the serpent enters into a relationship with The Breast, an apparatus emerges linking together previously generated alpha elements with ever greater sophistication. Wilfred worked out a grid by which one can follow the elements getting organized eventually into an algebraic cal-culus. That's as unfamiliar to me as sasanquas and osmunds, I must confess, but fundamentally an algebraic calculus is no different in its function than is a story. Each organizes alpha elements into patterns designed to generate meaning."

Several times Sakutarô shakes his head carefully.

"I have the impression you're trying to clear your head so that you can think."

He nods assent ever so slightly. At least I think he does.

"Now here's the mystery. In our Adam and Eve story, God expressly forbids pursuing knowledge. Try it, and you get the death penalty. Today you describe a fish sneaking under a woman's kimono and coupling with the breast. Like it's committing a crime."

Sakutarô raises his hand to stop me from going on. It's about time he shuts me up.

The illusory realms Gautama saw. A night of gorgeous moonlight where luxuriant tropical trees intermesh their greens, where lovely swells lap the shore—there the yearned for path to religiosity was revealed.

"Religiosity evokes the gorgeous and the grand. By con-trast, illumination by mind, both in its vitalizing and structuring powers, reveals detail, such as particularizing vegetable life and sets up patterns referring to the real world and not to illusory realms."

Surely, tender affections coursed through his heart and his eyes mirrored the illusions of immortality. Those eyes moreover brightly illuminated the bliss of seeing one's delusions and their dubious silhouettes fade dejectedly away. Oh, how it tints the twilight of my wretched life to think of him, to sense the illusory realms he saw!

He shouts out with unmistakable derision,

Gautama! I love both the illusory lotus petals that you saw and the aromas of fevered blossoms capable of blooming in ashen lives. O, Gautama, what excessively ostentatious solitude!

"Cicero observed no nation or people every existed without religion. And Bion insisted...."

He sits up and cups his ear, thrusting his head toward a corner of the room.

Hear music playing somewhere! Organ melodies aromatic on the evening air—dismal, pathetic, oppressive airs.

He strains more intently and repeats, listening afresh.

Dismal pathetic oppressive airs. Play on, whoever sits at the keyboard in that distant church. Play the organ. Play the organ. Play the organ. Pull all the stops, all the stops, in that huge black organ.

He gets up and strides to the corner, a man on a mission. Sternly he demands,

Ah, who in these pitch-black depressing glooms plays that awesome, that gigantic organ at one with the wall? The fervent passions and shudders of religion, the spasms of the pipe organ—a requiem!

He reaches out both arms, imploringly.

Pray, you who are afflicted. There's nothing to fear, there's no time for fear. Play the organ!

He turns away from the wall and gazes out the window. He stands motionless.

Before daybreak I hear a cock crowing from beyond the city's doors. It's Mother's tremolo summoning me from her forsaken country patch.

Barely audible, he crows,

Tow-tay-kuur, Tow-roo-mour, Tow-roo-mour. **My soul flutters its wings this morning on its chilly cot. The scenery I can see through gaps in the shutters seems everywhere joyfully radiant. Before daybreak, however, a singular despondency slinks slyly toward my bed. It's the cock's crow coming over dim treetops to summon me from its far-off country patch.**

Now he crows loudly,

Tow-tay-kuur, Tow-roo-mour, Tow-roo-mour.

"A reinforced crowing summons you out of bed and into the daylight, mother's tremolo conjoined with the lusty energy of a rooster. In our story, it's Eve coupled with the serpent. Wake up! Get on with it! Eat of the Tree of Knowledge. Stop playing that lugubrious organ music. 'Up lad,' comes the summons from A. E. Housman. 'Morns abed and daylight slumber were not meant for man alive.'"

He turns to me and smiles, the evidence of his recent drunkenness mysteriously evaporated. He returns to the couch, sits down and looks at me in the friendliest fashion.

Naturally, my problems remain unresolved. These are, however, matters of setting my personal affairs on a solid base. Marriage remains an issue for the far-off future, so I'll set it aside together with every gloom—lay it there on fate's garbage heap.

He looks past me and out the window.

All forms of depression are unnatural and pathological ways to live—every depression a blighted, jaded illusion. That black organ blankets my ardors.

"As does alcohol."

He gets up and walks out. I am furious with myself for that last statement. Talk about playing a black organ. Utterly gratuitous. An insult to his intelligence. All right, don't go pathological. So it goes. Win some. Lose some. Besides, it was an amazing conversation. Wouldn't Wilfred have gotten a kick out of it!

NOTES FROM ABOVEGROUND

Sakutarô wrote to friends that he found himself a satchel of contradictions and inconsistencies—decadent yet searching for the truth, simultaneously mystic and materialist. He's surely candid!

Her milky, long, and always richly moistened nape

This describes a geisha or entertainer, a woman trained in the arts of male titillation.

Gautama! I love both the illusory lotus petals that you saw

Gautama taught that humankind's major source of suffering is attachment to desire, whether for sex, fame or whatever. Although Gautama had freed himself of desire, Sakutarô depicts him observing "illusory realms." Does Gautama experience the same libidinous urges that trouble the poet? Phrases like "gorgeous moonlight" and "luxuriant tropical trees" intermeshing their greens subtly eroticize Gautama's thinking.

Before daybreak I hear a cock crowing

Roosters, figures of manliness and swagger, announce the dawn, thus telling lover boy it's time to go home. Their crowing magically expels the night's demons—including licentiousness and drunkenness. The poet links this cock with his mother, the voice of his conscience.

Ah, that poor-hearted girl in the dreams I have these days

This elegy is for Elena. "Poor hearted" echoes the biblical notion from the Beatitudes that those who are "poor in spirit" or humble-minded are blessed.

I pace quietly back and forth over the carpet in a spacious room

Carpets and spaciousness imply an exotic setting available only to the wealthy.

NOTES FROM UNDERGROUND

Sakutarô comes in, plainly dressed. He makes a beeline for the couch.

Ranges glitter the sky. Blizzards whiten the peaks. The roads here have worsened recently, slush turning to mud.

"Reminds me of alcohol turning your mind to mush recently."
He replies, with unmistakable sobriety,

This somber city of my birth! Mount Akagi looms over Saigawa, over rows of shoulder-to-shoulder houses, over that fire-watch tower, over eaves already decorated with pine.

Pause.

Let me tell you about my town.

"It's your turn to tell us a story."

Let me tell you about the place of my birth. I love to walk alone through the back lanes of Mukaichô. I love watching country bumpkins throng the intersections. Far removed from the crowds, I go up to the drying platform on our roof and look at the sky, the moon, the stars, the sun or at pine groves.

"With your brain dried out, you can think. You name things. Whether slugs, snakes, lizards, or the sun, the moon and the stars."

On rare occasions I see an airplane.

He shifts his position. I sense a sea-change in his state of mind.

Winds from Akagi, blow. Blow! Oh, listen to the humming of children's kites! I watch everything—shadowed by a friendless fate.

Sakutarô begins to moan. I am startled. Where's he coming from? His moaning continues, communicating unmistakable sorrow. Alpha elements. I hardly dare to breathe, caught up spellbound in his story. Alpha-function. He weeps.
Through staccato gulpings of grief, I hear,

The ardent depressions I repeatedly dedicate to you. Ah, my irresistible love—your tubercular fevers!

He turns to the wall, bowing his head, hands clasped in prayer.

My love! When sun sets today I'll stop by your place and leave a kiss on that dark door. Have mercy on the one who weeps dejectedly in the depths of his self.

He is unable to continue.

"I am reminded of St. Peter's denial and Judas Iscariot's betrayal. You know the story. It gets told something like this: Peter began to curse and to swear, saying, 'I know not this man of whom ye speak.' And the Lord turned and looked upon Peter, and Peter remembered the word of the Lord, 'Before the cock crow twice, thou shalt deny me thrice.' And Peter went out and wept bitterly.

"I suggest mindfulness has hurled you into unbearable depression, as you recognize within yourself a proclivity for ruthlessness and selfishness, evidenced in your behavior toward the tubercular, dying Elena. Recently you drove awareness away through alcohol. Today you are stone-cold sober, swamped with unbearable insight, agonizing in the depths of what Klein identified as the depressive position."

He touches the wall with his hands, like a blind man trying to recognize a face by touch,

Out of compassion, will you tell me about the path to eternity?

"When St. Peter recognized his betrayal, he wept bitterly. When Judas recognized he had sold out his Lord for 30 pieces of silver, he hanged himself, a path to eternity. Recognizing your behavior toward the fevered Elena, you are overwhelmed with grief. Will you deal with your recognition by weeping and requesting forgiveness, or will you be

torn by such suffering that you have no out but to commit
suicide?"

He sobs, his entire body wracked with spasms of grief. In
a state of self-awareness this powerful, I remind myself it is
critical not to violate what Bion called "Isolation." I get what
Sakutarô is experiencing—sort of! He is utterly naked and
as vulnerable as one can imagine. If I barge into his
Isolation, he might never again risk that level of vulnerability. What we have here is a deep paradox—I have to let
Sakutarô know I'm getting what he's experiencing while
making it plain I can't.

Sounding like a great organ far away, he intones,

**You alone know the agonies of human emptiness. You
alone know, yes, you know these gloomy purple passions.**

Tears begin to stream down my face. Christ! I give thanks
to Freud for inventing the couch.

Sakutarô rolls back on his back. Long silence. He sits up.
He mimes removing a cap and flipping it aside.

**I remove my cap and flip it aside. Ah, memories.
Dreadfully shredded memories. Miserable memories that
fester in shame.**

He falls back on the couch. Another sea-change in his
state of mind.

**From under pliant grasses, aroused passions waken to
spring with dazzle and vigor. Vernal feelings blissfully and
buoyantly sting his heart with spring.**

I say gently, "Your work as a writer is an unremitting
effort to know the workings of your mind, as you told us

long ago. It is this curiosity that drives you to come to these sessions, terrible as the truth can be. The fact you choose to do this work may be the greatest mystery, since lying and evasions and denial and alcohol and such are so easily available to spare you the suffering you're experiencing."

Yes, rejuvenating thoughts are, more than anything, like snow that melts on a day in spring.

In words hushed with adoration, he adds,

One senses in nature those blissfully buoyant throbs of sex in a heart at the height of its powers.

"Isn't that astonishing!" I reply. "The *truth* of your sexual life with Elena—in all its power and terror—brings you to the height of your powers."

I feel life's silent flow break through the doldrums of benumbed thought. Like water warming perceptibly at the bottom of a bog where agonies are too deeply depressing, I sense the teary-eyed and hesitant arrival of spring.

He leaves. It's my turn to get a tissue and wipe my eyes. I'm feeling overwhelmed. For the first time it seems I glimpse what Melanie really means by depression. As Wilfred might say, "Now, that's the depressive position!"

You see, it is the first day of creation.

Notes from Aboveground

After turning thirty-one in November 1917, Sakutarô felt increasing pressure from parents and friends to marry. Sakutarô thirsted for steady sex but, still deeply conflicted by his love for Elena who had died that May, he was ill-prepared to make a commitment. Unemployed and unemployable, he had no way short of his father's dependable generosity to support a wife. Then, too, his family didn't want him bringing home another "social disease."

He needed a sexual outlet, so everyone agreed on an arranged marriage. The "winning" candidate was not much of a beauty, he said, but then she wasn't ugly either. It was all right as long as she wasn't homely; he couldn't imagine wanting sex with an unattractive woman. From the outset, Sakutarô had no illusions about why he tied the knot. After the ceremony, the newlyweds lived in the Hagiwara mansion. Their first child, a girl who became a dancer and writer, was born in September 1919. In October Dr. Hagiwara retired and the entire family moved from the hospital.

Sakutarô wrote to friends that he found that the Bible was not only thought-provoking but also a lyric poem loaded with images that inspired fresh ideas. He compared his reactions to reading Scripture with Nietzsche's works. He found them as poetic as they were philosophical.

Let me tell you about my town,
about the pine groves on Mount Akagi's summit

What he doesn't tell us is that the dominant social value of Maebashi was that "sameness" guaranteed harmony and social stability. Simple-minded folk feared what bad luck a maverick might bring the polity. Sakutarô loved to put on his student's black cape and roam through the shabby areas on Maebashi's northern fringes. There he stopped at dingy bars to drink alone and gaze at the ranges to the north.

I go up to the drying platform on our roof

Rooftop laundry drying platforms save space and allow relatively unshaded exposure to sunlight. He enjoyed retreating to the platform to remove himself from the family. These platforms provide the poet with a metaphor for his sense of isolation. He is the distant observer fated to live a miserable existence in a backward provincial city. Once again he converts the functional to the symbolic.

Ah, my irresistible love—your tubercular fevers

The referent is Elena, who died from pulmonary tuberculosis almost a year before this poem appeared. Sakutarô often biked or took the train to the next city where she lived and pestered her at her home. Alerting her to his presence by whistling or tossing stones, he insisted that she drop whatever she was doing and visit with him.

I'll stop by your place and leave a kiss on that dark door

It isn't just twilight darkening the door. Recall that Elena had been a "shade" almost a year when this poem appeared.

You alone know the agonies of human emptiness

Nobody, not even the poet, could know despair better than a dying twenty-four-year-old mother and wife.

From under pliant grasses
aroused passions waken

Sakutarô dedicated this poem, "Radiant Soul," to Shimazaki Tôson (1872-1943) on his fiftieth birthday. Historians and critics designate Tôson the first poet to make a successful break from classical verse to new forms of poetry. Sakutarô hopes that this admired poet, a man who had just survived a scandalous love affair with a niece, might find renewed inspiration, hope and creative energy in the coming of spring. "Radiant Soul" heads a section of five poems that deal with spring's bewitching and erotic nature.

Notes from Underground

Sakutarô doesn't show up. A blank envelope lies on the chair in my waiting room with a check covering the sessions, including this one, the last day of the month. This happened once before. I am immediately filled with foreboding. Is he putting his affairs in order prior to committing suicide?

I remember with horror his asking me, "Out of compassion will you tell me about the path to eternity?" I strain for sounds of his arrival. Nothing. I can't keep anyone from committing suicide, but why did I have to be so blunt and point out Elena was a dying twenty-four-year-old wife and mother when he treated her so shabbily and ruthlessly!

Besides, who says I can't keep someone from committing suicide! Not the law. My colleague had to pay a family a million dollars for not preventing a patient's suicide. I can hear the indictment, "Of course you can prevent suicide. It's your job." Well, why did some ten patients on suicidal observation in Los Angeles psychiatric hospitals—twenty-four hours a day surveillance by a huge staff—kill themselves while in hospital in the past decade alone?

Yes, but did I have to cut him to pieces when he arrived hung over? Hold on, isn't that what a surgeon does? I must be cruel only to be kind. Is Sakutarô's predicament of the mind any less threatening to his life than whatever brings someone to major surgery?

The dismaying truth is I can't prevent suicide. No one can. Not even a small army of dedicated hospital workers. Suppose every suicidal person knows this, but I circumvent this terrible truth by insisting my partner sign a contract not to kill himself, at least without telling me first? If I'm that stupid—or that blatant about covering my backside—how can anyone take anything I say seriously?

Awful as it sounds, I am not—can't be—responsible for Sakutarô's life. I don't doubt folks may hear this as a callousness bordering on the criminal. A betrayal of my responsibility. Here I offer to take Sakutarô through an exploration of his psyche and yet disregard the responsibility of that journey. I'm abandoning thereby my ultimate humanity, namely, I am my brother's keeper. Instead, I flip off my responsibility as easily as Sakutarô flipped off that imaginary cap. As his protector, parent and guide, with him on the brink of despair, don't I throw him a rope and hold tight?

The lamentable fact is I can't. If forty or so members of a hospital staff can't, how can I? When do I sleep? Exercise? Sit in the garden and sip wine? How can I stay on duty twenty-four hours a day? Besides, that doesn't work either. Check with the various hospitals currently being sued in Los Angeles. I am not responsible for the facts of life. I am responsible for submitting to them.

I hear someone in the waiting room. I feel giddy with

relief. I go out and it's two kids selling cookies. "No!" I snap and slam the door on them. I trot out some old hat. One can't move to a new world without, willy-nilly, destroying the old one. Adam and Eve couldn't have knowledge and innocent nudity at the same time. They got booted out of Eden, a big angel with a flaming sword, as I remember, preventing their return. Growth is not the same as a reversible perspective. Now you see the vase. Now you see the face.

No, Adam, you can't see genitals the same way ever again. Innocence? Poof! Gone! Somebody said one can't ever recapture preconceptual innocence. That's been my experience. Worlds in collision! You want to change? Move to another part of the planet? It's not for the faint-hearted. There's no going back. That big angel with the flaming sword. And no assurance of safe passage.

NOTES FROM ABOVEGROUND

Only lyrics from the soul can transform experience into art that speaks meaningfully to the modern human being. Sakutarô insists that verse must refer to the psychic pain of alienation. For a millenium, vastly different concerns had ruled native poetry. Japanese expected a bard to create either verbal "charm" or tear-squeezing comments on the ephermality of life, love and beauty. Instead, Sakutarô aimed at communicating the terrors of his alienated and empty life. He was uninterested in presenting a neatly oriented and centered map of his mind—or anything that might match traditional definitions of "pretty."

Free of conventional expectations, Sakutarô avoided either tickling his readers' ears or feeding them metaphorical candy. He never thought his task was to make readers "happy." He took a perverse pleasure in buffeting them with verse that was unlike anything they had ever read—the unadorned, distressing and tormenting howls of one man's psyche. This amounted to a revolutionary bludgeoning.

Sakutarô's style and content conveyed the shock of total freshness. His early verse stripped away the artificial facades of traditional nature-centered poetry, verse that had lulled generations of readers—and even the militarists!—into believing that as long as people relate to nature they will remain spiritually "whole." Fearlessly unmasking his soul, Sakutarô encouraged readers to look for universal mental states. Recognizing through the poet's experiences their own despair, frustrations, aloneness and self-contradictory views, they might learn to deal with or come to terms with themselves.

Sakutarô had no use for the chummy, tribal and non-confrontational approach of classical verse. His revolutionary language and themes blaringly proclaimed that the modern epoch had arrived. His verse howls: *Banzai! Banzai! Banzai!*

NOTES FROM UNDERGROUND

No Sakutarô. The fact he had paid for last month's sessions by leaving that check in the waiting room had given me not only anxiety about suicidality but also hope. Alas, hope deferred breaketh the heart. After two weeks I dropped him a note stating I no longer was keeping his time. He did not reply. Winter passed, a dry, sunshine-drenched winter, the littoral Mediterranean climate of southern California. Sakutarô passed from my thoughts.

Then, on the first day of spring, Sakutarô sent a terse letter; he wanted to resume the work. I wrote back, reminding him we had the issue of payment for the sessions I had kept before terminating our working arrangement. Who was responsible for those two weeks? He sent payment by return mail. I was delighted. Of course, hope blooms eternal. He comes in as though no time has elapsed since our last session. He does not greet me.

He lies down and says matter-of-factly,

You've come to the impoverished countryside. Energies depleted, you sit all day on a ridge between the paddies and poke the tip of your spindly umbrella at the dead frog that shares the paddy ridge with you. Your thoughts are particularly gloomy today—anguished and tormented by the oppressive thirsts you feel in this swamp. However replenish your emptiness?

"That's what brings you back—a need for replenishment. Maintaining the fitness of one's soul is as relentless a task as maintaining the fitness of one's body. Entropy is grandly indifferent, pervading every nook and cranny of all life— although sometimes it seems to carry on an especially nasty vendetta against spiritual life. At any rate, even God rested on the seventh day, presumably replenishing his spiritual stores."

Hang up a portrait of my hand. Hang it on walls far and wide.

"'Replenish my energies!' you urge us, 'so I can resume my writing.'" He gathers himself together, indicating enough with preliminaries.

Sketching out a great circle with both hands, he intones,

Frozen, overcast winter skies layer a terribly depressing landscape. There the figure of a woebegone, dejected, sallow horse fated to causality silently eats grass along the road.

"Fated to causality?"

Fated to causality!

he repeats, annoyed.

It appears to look at me.

Then, in full gallop of annoyance, he snaps,

Oh, hurry, shake a leg and be off! I want to believe in my own "free will."

"What about the sallow horse?"

Listen, horse! Expunge your sallow shadow from the dry plate of this woebegone, hopeless, frozen solid, causally-fated formulaic scene.

"I appreciate you're eager to get on with our work now that you're back, but 'causally-fated formulaic scene...'?" He stops me by holding up both hands.
Then he asks in straightforward fashion, without a hint of pretentiousness,

How do you suppose I might refashion my present feelings and divert them from reflecting drearily on my milieu or my past?

I find his no-nonsense directness endearing. I'm tickled he's back.

What I've lost particularly in life is only my contentment. But, oh, it's been lost for far too long.

"You want to believe in your own free will. Yes, sir! You're not a sallow horse or a woebegone, dejected sallow drunk! No more formulaic scenes like we endured last winter, with wholly predictable, melodramatic, lugubrious, causally-fated drunken rubbish. You want to wipe out that sallow shadow from the dry plate of your memory and mind. Well, then, shake a leg and get on with it! If that's what you are proposing, I'm all for it."

He smiles. The game is on.

Near a quiet path through the field a dismal electric light glows late into the night. Nearby hills teem with huge trees: varieties of oak, cypress, beech, and zelkova—their foliage lush and richly dense. I see clouds of moths gather and swarm together and then head for that single dismal light. Like terrifying hordes of locusts, throngs of tiny bugs reel round the light, grow giddy, jam together. Die. Moths flutter their weighty wings as they sense the awesome agonies of sex deep within that dismally florid light.

I experience a wonderful giddiness. It happened time and again when talking with Wilfred. Bion evoked in me an endless back-and-forth between paranoid-schizoid and depressive positions. He'd say something and a light wouldn't go on. Quite the opposite. I'd feel my mind blown and shaken. Only by-and-by—sometimes "by-and-by" meaning months and even years—did his words slam together in a marvelous revealing coherence. Of course I was depressed at my slow uptake, but once past that, sheer joy. Which I experience this very moment listening to Sakutarô, who also possesses a first-rate mind.

I see moth wings substantial as pound cake. I see doleful, isolated lives wasted by their cravings.

"Given the insubstantialness of thought, how is one to oppose unimaginably heavy instinctual forces? This is precisely the problem Freud addressed in *Civilization and Its Discontents*. Our thinking apparatus is so frail when it comes to dealing with the awesome agonies of sex, little wonder so many doleful, isolated lives get wasted by instinctual cravings. I suggest you discovered that isolating yourself these many months from our work put you at spiritual risk. The Good Book notes man cannot live by bread alone but by the word. Let me hasten to add this work is just another kind of effort against the ravages of instinctual forces. Many roads lead to Rome. Not all, however."

I think of the impenetrable mysteries that populate the forlorn instincts that everything alive inherits—those perpetually and permanently desolate, those so florid feelings.

He laughs. Out loud. Totally unexpected. What fun. And then he starts telling a story.

Strolling through a pine grove, I noted at a spot far removed from city streets a cheerful looking café secluded in a grove. Without a single customer. The setup features a young girl just awakening to passion. She brings in my special order—refreshing as the dawn.

He pantomimes,

I lift my fork sedately, eat my omelet, the fries, the rest.

He makes a burp, patting his full tummy.

—my exceedingly genteel tastes.

"Well, with service like that, who wouldn't feel cheerful! Go instincts!"

He sits up and turns to me. It feels completely collegial.

Is ideology a unified design?

He looks past me, following his thought.

Meditating under that tree in a densely luxuriant forest, Gautama sensed the colorless clarity of nature. As he developed his single-minded ideology and quickened his meditative focus, he perceived how he could utterly dissolve into Nirvana.

"You have just talked about the complexity of nature, and its terrifying hordes of locusts, throngs of tiny bugs, moth wings as substantial as pound cake in their vast number. You recognize impenetrable mysteries that populate the forlorn instincts all life inherits. I suggest your appreciation for complexity contrasts starkly with the single-minded ideology of Gautama. He reduces nature to what's colorless and clear. From this reductionism Gautama manages an ideology of unified design. Bion considered such reductionism a stripping away of reality, a denudation. Gautama denudes the densely luxuriant real world. This simplifying enables him to dissolve utterly into Nirvana."

As he trod over moonbeams, Gautama asked his good-natured mind: "Is ideology a unified design?"

"Complexities do not inspire a good-natured mind. They persecute us most painfully, stirring up dreadful anxieties. Considering epistemology from an evolutionary perspective, ignorance goes against nature. I have to judge immediately whether that patch of yellow waving in the bush is a tiger or a tiger lily. Whenever something unexpected happens, I conjure up at least four theories to account for it before I blink.

"Happens automatically. Does for all of us. I call it 'Condemned to Plausibility,' the single greatest enemy of truth. It's been wired into our brain over millions of years. We can't take our time in making judgments. We have to act now, coming up with a plausible hypothesis. In short, human brains are biologically driven by a need for an ideology that unifies design. We're all wired this way. Melanie was right when she called a state of disunity and confusion—a state of ignorance, if you will—paranoid-schizoid. Absolutely. Here is the great conundrum: we're supposed to make our way in the world by learning, yet we confront a "shake a leg and be off" state deep in the very wiring of our one hundred billion neurons. If we can't tolerate a world with no unified design, how can we learn from experience? You want to walk over moonbeams? No problem. Anything for a good-natured mind."

What has Adam recalled of his deplorable daytime yearnings? Like clouds, like infinitely compassionate love, primordial feelings float far beyond the shores of memory—wholly impossible to grasp.

I blink, startled by the originality of his question. "Adam named all the animals. That is hard work. Creating a nomenclature isn't exactly a romp in the park. Or over moonbeams. It's deplorably difficult. Takes mindfulness. Why do you, like Adam, engage in this deplorable work of mindfulness when like Gautama, you can pleasantly spin out ideology? Why do you write? Why do you come back today?"

He looks directly at me again, his face now taut and drawn. I hear myself saying, "You spoke of a woebegone, dejected horse fated to causality. Is our learning disability inexorably decreed? Is it in fact asking too much of us to tolerate a lack of closure? We want to believe in our own free will, or are we evolutionarily condemned to a hopeless, frozen solid, formulaic scene?"

Time is up. When he leaves, I am astonished to find myself deeply depressed. Hits me like a ton of bricks.

NOTES FROM ABOVEGROUND

Sakutarô took a two-year vacation from poetry between August 1919 and October 1921. Regular mandolin concerts, family responsibilities, and an arts symposium he convened for local poets demanded his energies. Aside from being the official sponsor of the symposium, Sakutarô lectured on the principles of modern poetry. The poets met fifteen times in Maebashi's library.

You've come to the impoverished countryside

Sakutarô feels his prospects are poor because he lives in a backward province. Provincial values are quicksand to whatever is new or different—no chance for life there.

Fated to causality

This implies karma, that is, the horse—poet—is destined to reap what it—he—sows.

Expunge your sallow shadow from the dry plate

An avid photographer, Sakutarô implies he controls the "reality" he photographs. One of the poet's favorite themes is that fate and causality undermine free will. More than anything he would like to deal with life as a photographer who can arbitrarily wipe reality clean. Thereby he could erase the karmic results of his behavior.

How he could utterly dissolve into Nirvana

Annihilating desires by dissolving into Nirvana appealed

to Sakutarô. Unlike Gautama, though, he knew he couldn't manage the feat, and he envied anyone who could.

**At a spot far removed from city streets
a cheerful looking café secluded in a grove**

No walk-in traffic here—what an unlikely place for any restaurant! The café serves as a metaphor for the poet's disengagement from society.

Session
Never to a Bar Again
31

NOTES FROM UNDERGROUND

Sakutarô arrives on time, but he looks hung over. He walks to the couch unsteadily. He closes his eyes and lies perfectly still. "Are you sleeping?" I ask. Without opening his eyes, he retorts lazily,

On this most tranquil bed, a singularly mighty and serene emotion lulls my soul into a sound sleep. That sentiment curbs passion's potent agonies and makes me forget my vain resistance to fate, my uneasy feelings about life, my fretful impatience.

I remember Jesus remaining silent before Caiaphas, the high priest. Jesus grasped instantly the fact he'd get a better hearing talking to a wall. You lose credibility if you don't realize when you're wasting you breath. I say nothing. Time passes.

He says sleepily,

Like an organ playing a requiem, black feelings boil up. Ah, waves of passion, waves of free will, waves of evil intentions. Waves! Waves! Waves! Waves of unutterably gloomy melancholy. You know, I'll be contemplating the deathless time of nature and thinking of the ocean mirrored in Gautama's forsaken clock.

I say nothing. Time passes.
He sits straight up, his feet remaining on the couch.

Forlorn and sinking into depression, I cross the footbridge. Where now the singular sentiment that resolutely rejects compromise and any easy solution? I cross the footbridge desolately alone, carrying that singular black shadow wrapped in my cape.

He takes a deep breath, punctuating each phrase with his forefinger.

The shadow abhors all things. Pulverizes all things. Rebels against all things. Ridicules all things. Demolishes all things. Feels hostility toward all things.

He falls back on the couch.

Surely I have very special talents. And yet there is simply no special *work* on Earth these days that matches my abilities. Rather than accept work not commensurate with my skills, let me leap far beyond the orbit of the Earth.

"I suggest your leap beyond the orbit of earth is fueled by alcohol."

The transparent remorse one feels on the morning after

coming home dead drunk. Recollections of nothing less than boorish and asinine behavior: embarrassing acts, excessively obscene and absolutely contemptible comportment in the darkness. The truth is that on the morning of the hangover the mere thought of alcohol simply makes you feel like throwing up. *I'll never go to a bar again.*

He sits up again and shouts,

I'll never go to a bar again! Never, as along as I live, never to repeat what caused these annoying regrets.

He swings his feet on the floor and launches into an account of the Battle of Waterloo. Several times he makes eye contact with me, then turns away and lectures on. He finishes his history lesson and walks out, still unsteady on his pins.

Every conversational partner wants to shut us up. Why? Very simple—pain! The Unpleasure Principle! If you're a decent sort to start with—and everyone who continues the work is—then you don't want the dark stuff to come to life. Hurts too much.

St. Paul insists love never faileth. Doth not behave itself unseemly. Thinketh no evil. Beareth all things, believeth all things, hopeth all things, endureth all things.

I'll buy that. Except it's only half the story—Eros. The mind simultaneously abhors, pulverizes, rebels, ridicules, demolishes—in sum, feels hostility toward all things—Thanatos.

Damn that alcohol!

NOTES FROM ABOVEGROUND

These prose works appeared in 1922. By this time Sakutarô had extracted as much inspiration as he could from Christian sources. He now looks into Buddhism, nihilism and intellectual history for fresh ideas to pummel into poetry. Only concepts that resonate with his emotions interest him. Historical events did not affect his thought and writing. Let newspapers deal with quotidian matters. Marxist poets wrote of the suffering masses, noted increasing surveillance, and complained of the militarization of their society. Meanwhile, Sakutarô's poetry remained oblivious to the momentous historical events developing around him.

The ocean mirrored in Gautama's forsaken clock

The sea is endless and endlessly boring—a figure for the eternal. It is as well the mother of creation and a symbol of the unfathomable psyche. It implies the totality of visible reality, life, the unconscious. "Forsaken clock" implies changeless existence beyond time. Meditation nurtures spiritual calm—alien to this poet but something he ardently desired.

Forlorn and sinking into depression, I cross the footbridge

Crossing a span of any kind symbolizes the wish to escape one's painful reality and enter into another realm filled with promise and joyous dreams.

Hagiwara Sakutarô, Late 1930s

PART IV

Brain or Mind?

NOTES FROM UNDERGROUND

Sakutarô misses the next three sessions. Once again I register uneasiness, playing over and over in my mind's ear that stunning Pauline litany—his singular black shadow abhorring and pulverizing and demolishing and ridiculing. Had such tremendous insight blasted him to kingdom come?

What brings most folks scurrying for help, and to my couch, is they suffer too much insight. "I don't know why that bothers me so much, but it's driving me crazy," they fret in great pain.

As I've said before, doing the work sounds simple. "Say what's on your mind." Until you try it. Fiendishly difficult. Thoughts circle round and round like giant California condors until they crash-land on the couch.

There they strut in your face. Bigger than life. As vivid as sex. Threatening. Embarrassing. One scary surprise after another popping up from nowhere and Boo! flapping noisily.

Knock! Knock! Knock! Sakutarô shows up. Whenever a partner arrives that always gives me relief. I know, it shouldn't. No memory. No desire. OK, no one's perfect. He knocks three or four times more before I ever get to the waiting room. I guess he's drunk. Wrong. He's stone-cold sober but everything about him "too much"—eyes too bright, face flushed, body tense and coiled.

Cracking an imaginary whip in my face, he shouts,

I urge the gasping horses on!

When he lands on the couch, he keeps cracking the whip.

Sunday morning: As I spur my two gleaming stallions, my light carriage dashes over a tree-lined suburban road.

Crack! Crack! Crack! I feel puny and scared, pitted against his break-neck disturbance. Suddenly his arms freeze in mid-motion. Statue-still he asks quietly,

On second thought, isn't everything perhaps the exact opposite of my description? Isn't this rather a stifling setting where we find a bogged-down dray? And a testily impatient wagoner whose nags will not budge?

Then he takes off again. Crack! Crack! Crack! In full gallop he turns around and roars,

How does that strike you, thinker!

I raise my eyebrows and open wide my eyes. He lies back down, exhausted. When I've gathered my thoughts, I suggest quietly, "Your second state of mind is the exact opposite of your first."

Before a thought becomes perfectly packaged, you see, we have day after day of depressing weather when indecisive expressions refuse to move on.

He sings,

Should auld acquaintance be forgot,
And never brought to mind?
Should auld acquaintance be forgot,
And days of auld lang syne?

With sudden sadness, nodding his head up and down, he offers,

I'd love to sit like a seal on an ice floe where, under a show of northern lights, I can absent-mindedly "forget myself." There endless ages will pass by. With no clear-cut night and day in the region of the aurora borealis, the light at sundown dissipates dimly and morosely.

"I suggest you feel deeply split—simultaneously urging your gleaming stallions on at full gallop and at the same time you're a wagoner whose broken-down nag won't budge. You've told us you want to understand the workings of your mind. This ambition drives your life—but contradictions within yourself make this impossible. You experience incompatible states of mind simultaneously. This violates the law of contradiction, a logical absurdity. Its irreconcilability leaves you split and torn, and it registers as madness."

Bridge Out!

he roars,

Who knows the bridge is out? My soul is streaking, streaking, streaking toward its tragic end.

"Precisely," I interject quickly. "You can't bridge your two states of mind. One comfort is that, in fact, we do know the bridge is out."

He jumps to his feet.

Gales...gales...heavy seas...heavy seas!

Cupping his hands, he shouts into the storm,

Secure the portholes... Secure the portholes. Waves... Waves... Waves! Batten the hatches! Batten the hatches!

Shielding his eyes, he peers into the distance.

Dreadful mountain. I saw the hulk of a dreadful mountain spewing smoke into night's jet-black skies. The scene reminded me of the eye of a gigantic spider. Flickering its red tongue and crawling about like a crab, it stretched out its legs and crept over the foothills. Looming directly ahead, that grotesque hulk stood poised to consume me.

He jerks his head and stares at me, eyes too wide open. I realize with a start he is dreadfully ill. His face has now sagged, the corners of his mouth drooping, the fiery intensity with which he had arrived blown out like a candle. Brain ill. He is spiraling into the bottomless pit of Melancholia.

Staring blankly at the ceiling, he says,

Her chilled, pallid face reflected an elegantly gleaming

and comely moon. The moon's visage mortified. Letting tears stream I daub her lips with blood. Oh, how I ache for her! I cling to and trifle with her departed soul. Gentle burial songs meander gloomily through pussy willow shadows that stir in evening wind.

"You've become ill," I say gently. "Emotionally ill. Brain ill."

Laid out to imitate the living, this body had been beautifully, mournfully and bewitchingly tinted. Her chest, her lips, her face, her arms—ah, moistened everywhere with brushes and balm. Oh, cherished May corpse! As I writhe before you like a gold-green snake, I sense that some secretion had stuck to me, and so I wipe my skin on the carpet of *death*.

He rallies himself. With a wave of his hand, he tosses out dismissively,

I'm a rustic chicken. I flap my wings in the yard of a poor peasant, fly over his fence, then peck at shriveled bugs. I'm a desolate rustic chicken.

He scratches his head.

This singularly odd impression perplexes me: once faith existed on the Earth. A fervent group of people gathered under the boundless immensity of cosmic space to seek that remote miracle of eternal life. Ah, where have they gone, where now their scattered fantasies? Demoralized memories drift like clouds in the blue.

He laughs feebly.

What a listless day! My fortunes become increasingly overcast and my cheerless, diseased depressions smolder under willow leaves.

"You have it exactly right," I tell him. "You have a diseased depression. Technically, it's called Melancholia, and that's an entirely different problem from depression caused by issues and conflicts within your mind."

He buries his face in his hands.

Wherever does a region this desolate exist?

"Maybe nowhere," I say. "It's possible there is no more anguished illness than Melancholia. Unspeakable. Unbearable."

This is how dusk approaches with an empty mind—merely a matter of unresponsive images vanishing like faint apparitions from a life of loneliness and loves.

"Melancholia empties the mind. It destroys your powers to think. Images appear, but you can't link them in a meaningful way. They simply vanish. We've talked about so-called alpha elements like words and alpha-function which links them into meaningful patterns. A mind too conflicted, a brain diseased—each destroys this power which enables you and me to put the world together into a coherent piece. Your old and dearest acquaintance, your mind, is now forgotten. A deadly secretion has stuck to your brain. It's called illness.

"Our brains are three pound physical organs, electrical in nature, and when the circuits misfire, illness follows. The brain is responsible for our behavior, moods and thinking. When the brain gets sick, these are precisely the functions affected. Physical illness *means* nothing, unlike the way The

Law of Contradiction means something in Logic, or the love of a mother for its infant is meaningful. Physical illness is a boring nuisance, that's what it is. It teaches us nothing. Adds nothing. A waste. Freud said of his jaw cancer, 'Most superfluous.' Bion differentiated suffering from pain. Suffering is a mind phenomenon whereas pain is a consequence of a physical problem. You're experiencing pain—a physical organ, your brain, is sick."

Whenever I take a rickshaw, panoramas open into the distance ahead and play desolately despondent flute songs that agitate feelings one would like to tolerate but can't. Yet see how intent my rickshaw man is on getting there!

And then he left. A wonderfully brave fellow! Tough. Like Freud. The pain dished out by a diseased brain is unaccountably terrible. Mood-disordered folks claim, nearly in unison, that no physical illness or surgery they have ever endured compares with the misery and anguish of an ill brain. In fact, that's why twenty-five percent find the pain unendurable and commit suicide.

What to do? Not a psychotropic medication on the horizon. Did the intensity of his work as a writer kindle the break-down? Possibly. That said, the fact remains: a brain illness is a physical problem, formally unrelated to the life of the mind. If the brain gets sick, that says no more about the mind—about the person—than does an illness of the liver.

So now what?

Notes from Aboveground

Should auld acquaintance be forgot

Sakutarô's answer, "Absolutely!" Spiritual renewal demands getting away from proprieties, one's immediate environment, habits, favorite thoughts and conventions.

Bridge Out!

Bridges, for Sakutarô, symbolize transitions to a realm where dreams can be realized. The train he's riding is a metaphor of his life, now hurtling toward hopelessness.

I saw the hulk of a dreadful mountain spewing smoke into night's jet-black skies

On clear days, Sakutarô could see Mt. Asama from his high school in Maebashi. Mt. Asama, the largest active volcano in Japan, never erupted lava during his lifetime, only smoke and ashes. Physical peril serves as a metaphor for a persistent sense of psychic jeopardy in the face of local conventions and cultural constrictions. No surprise, then, that as early as 1911, when he was twenty-four, Sakutarô had pleaded with his father for permission to live abroad—with a stipend of course! His father's answer: No!

Her chilled, pallid face reflected

The face is that of the long-dead Elena, whom he cannot erase from memory. While writing the poems for *Blue Cat*, Sakutarô felt he was living with her ghost.

Oh, cherished May corpse

Sakutarô indulges his fascination with caressing a female cadaver—Elena's? Oiling a corpse reflects his knowledge of alien customs, perhaps even New Testament practices. The Japanese do not embalm or prettify cadavers. The body is cremated soon after the wake.

Whenever I take a rickshaw

Neither commoners nor plebeians can afford this costly "limousine" service.

Session

Hallucinations and Lullabies

33

NOTES FROM UNDERGROUND

Sakutarô arrives in a terrible state. He has aged ten years and appears utterly uncared for. The wind goes out of my sails. What do I have to offer? Freud stressed the Unconscious is timeless. The human heart has not changed for thousands of years. We weep with Hecuba. We sulk with Achilles. Homer and Aeschylus and Virgil speak to us today as they've spoken to the race through thousands of years. When I agreed to talk with Sakutarô, I did so believing the tools available—language and mind— would prove adequate for the task.

Cheerfully and with confidence from many years of laboratory experience I journeyed back through time, meeting up with Sakutarô in the first decades of the twentieth century. We hit it off immediately, blissfully unaware a century separates us. Now, it has cracked open, revealing a vast gulf between us. The couch teeters on the edge of it, threatening our enterprise with ruin. Sakutarô's brain has fallen ill, and in this Year of our Lord 1922, I have nothing available to minister to a brain diseased. He and I can talk until we're blue in the face, and—I know in foresight—we'll not heal the faulty circuitry in his frontal lobes and emotional centers.

He lies down slowly. His dreadful vulnerability and my helplessness fill me with fear and trembling. How did the race survive without modern medicine? Without psychotropics? Without the option of Caesarean section? Without anesthesia! Explain that to me. I turn away. I remember my *Physicians Desk Reference* with its thousands of marvelous medicines, and I am awed by the achievement of the race in less than a hundred years.

Sakutarô speaks with great effort.

Depressions flap their wings and flit about my room. Ah, what apparitions! Absurdly indolent in this splendid weather, I shed desolate tears. After all, the ship of remembrance has already left port. This ghost-like season passes vaguely white, yet, ah, I see nothing. At least sing to me, you girls who were never loved!

"Melancholia prevents the brain from registering the outside world, however splendid. Days march by like indistinguishable ghosts. You can't remember ever being loved. Past and present pass into nothingness. The ship of life has left port."

A furious rainstorm drenched lamps along the street, distorting and flattening the scabby structures that lean into the hillside.

"A sick rain drenches the lamp of your mind. The darkness flattens the discrete structures of the world, making them all indistinguishable. Space, like time present and time past, has also passed into nothingness."

Someone's fate wanders soggy. Bundled in a huge caped coat, he gives the impression of a seedy, a scruffy black hawk. By then sopping wet—his shadow, his body, his life thoroughly sodden with grief.

He sits up on one elbow and addresses the wall.

Why have you come here? Oh, gentle, pallid shade eerie as grass, desolate ghost. Rotting fish reek from the shadows of your silhouette—the mournfully distressing and truly unbearable stench of grief. Only indescribable memories make my flesh creep and stand my hair on end. Oh, God! Unable by now to redeem those days, gnawing reflections make me wail on and on like a little child.

Tears stream down his face. He sits up and takes deep breaths, trying to calm himself. I am frantic. Surely there must be something I can do. I hear myself repeating his words, feebly, "like a little child."

He doesn't hear me, of course, as he now stares in horror at what surely is an apparition of his mind. In a hollow whisper he says,

A phantom-like cadaver lies under green-tinged Chinese pinks: black hair pouring to the floor, limbs flung out feebly, face-up on the bed. An eerily ashen lust, agonized by affecting musk and painfully, humiliatingly aware of the bounds of bewitching thoughts, steals in silently and surreptitiously from behind the closet curtains.

It hits me like a kick in the solar plexus—he is hallucinating.

Ah, near lamp-cast shadows on this spring night, it now delightedly sniffs at and toys with that body waxed by death: daubing oil on tender lips, fondling sleek white limbs. My love! since disturbing dreams coerce me, don't berate me for this pitiful fling!

"Mr. Hagiwara," I say with a hint of firmness. "You're having gnawing reflections like a little child. This is what I suggest. Lie back down on the couch, make yourself comfortable and pretend—and this is a pretty wild idea —pretend I'm singing a lullaby." He doesn't move. So I sing, "Lullaby. Da-da-da." And I hum the next few lines.

He looks at me and blinks. "You probably can't figure out which one of us is crazier, but here's my idea. I want to talk about psychosis. In your present state, I don't expect you to understand what I'm saying, but it's possible you will hear the words. What does a child hear when its mother talks and sings? I suspect benign and discrete elements that get stored in its head and over time get linked together in an increasingly sophisticated pattern. So I don't want you to think about what I'm saying. Simply listen. Let the words wash over you. By the way, I'm not going to sing. Just Zama Zama."

He is breathing normally. Not a flicker of emotion on his face. I wait. Then just like that he lies back down and becomes perfectly still. I start to talk. "A major finding in psychosis is a reversal in function of the sense apparatus. Ears don't hear voices. They produce voices. Eyes don't see what's out there. They project a scene, as we just witnessed with your visual hallucination about a body waxed with death. Freud worked with a woman who hallucinated smelling burnt pudding. This reversal of function is precisely what happens in dreams, but there one is sleeping. A psychosis is merely a wide-awake dream. In fact, you just noted that disturbing dreams coerce your hallucination. Precisely what Freud said."

He closes his eyes. Restfully. Who says we can talk until blue in the face and nothing will happen with his dreadful suffering? True, Sakutarô and I see darkly through a glass in nineteen hundred and twenty-two. Well, what about Galileo's dark glass? What would he make of the Hubble? What would Sakutarô and I make of psychosis four hundred years from now? I remember my *Physicians Desk Reference*. I remember St. Paul: *And now abideth faith and hope....*

He opens his eyes. I take their brightness a signal for me to continue. My words, though variegated as snowflakes, drift gently over him, their phonologic texture bearing comfort. Alpha elements *in statu nascendi*. I resume talking.

He stretches out on the couch. He looks years younger. He lies quietly until time is up. I talk the entire time. He gets off the couch slowly and comes over to me. I am not afraid. He takes my wrist gently and then my hand and looks at me long and hard. He gives a huge sigh and walks slowly to the door, looking back at me the whole while. I find it very touching. Surely Hamlet, supposedly mad, taking leave of Ophelia:

> *And with his head over his shoulder turned*
> *He seemed to find his way without his eyes,*
> *For out of doors he went without their help*
> *And to the last bended their light on me.*

Sakutarô is letting me know, despite his miserable psychosis, mind remains. Our conversation had comforted him, unwrinkling those cruel and sudden years branded on him by the illness. His madness had not transmogrified him into an alien! He still belonged to the human race, folks that sometimes come up with a Shakespeare or a Sakutarô.

Or a melancholic! Sometimes both at the same time. St. Paul points out in that chapter of Corinthians Sakutarô had paraphrased, humans can understand each other deeply and intimately. We are much more human than otherwise. Even psychosis can be made sense of. People get sick. Let's start there.

Sakutarô does not return. After much reflection, I choose not to contact him. Two weeks later, I cancel his sessions.

Notes from Aboveground

In May 1922 Sakutarô published a series of critical statements on tanka that fellow poets—if not critics and
scholars—rated highly for their rich insights and intuitions.
His wife was expecting their second child. He had grounds
for optimism, yet his poetry remained pessimistically
gloomy. He sounded like someone bolted to memories of his
earliest love, his mind mired in melancholy.

Session
A Gigantic Tsunami
34

NOTES FROM UNDERGROUND

Three months after our last session, Sakutarô sends me a note, short and to the point. He wants to resume our sessions. I remember how sick he had been and perhaps still is, so I make time immediately available. The next day we're back in business. He comes in, emaciated and worn, a grim survivor.

He lies down gingerly, breathing deeply in and out, apparently relieved to be back.

Look how my balloon rises lazily into the skies from a patch dense with summer grass. Knowing I'll be swept far beyond the globe's meridians, I've packed my lunar almanac in the basket.

There's a lilt to Sakutarô's voice. "Summertime. Lazy days. Happy days. I'm guessing that basket not only carries a lunar almanac—probably memories of your illness—but a picnic lunch as well. Your Melancholia drifts slowly beyond the globe's meridians."

My saké bottle's empty, so even the sot's gorgeous hallucinations are now but air.

"You've achieved sobriety. That's huge."

Little by little I'll leave terra firma behind. I'll let the vacuum of totally soundless space envelop me. Like this gas-inflated sphere, you see, I'm ascending lazily into the incomprehensibly desolate cosmos—absolutely alone.

"I suggest you descended happily onto the couch. You're returning to terra firma. I hear you shout, 'I'm back! And sober.' Your illness carried you away from this world and into a vacuum of totally soundless space, an incomprehensibly desolate cosmos."

Sakutarô turns his head this way and that, stretching luxuriously, finally snuggling into the couch. He looks the picture of contentment.

Like a fatuous gull I'll soar to the port's bustling flagstone streets strewn with shards of unglazed pottery. Pedestrians saunter aimlessly through dreary back streets dating from the 18th century. Blue, green and red banners flutter near old-fashioned bay windows capped with sheet-metal. How have streets with such profound sentiments survived?

"How has your mind survived? Your illness compressed time and space into nothingness. Now you notice every detail, even back streets with 18th century housing, banners fluttering near old-fashioned bay windows. The grave danger in Melancholia is suicide, taking the lives of twenty-five percent of those afflicted. The truly good news is that when recovery comes, you're as good as new."

Waving an arm and hand, he shouts out happily,

Ah, to whom shall I write my news?

Energy flows into him, and then with mock piety, folding his hands, he announces,

Way of the True Disciple—from a vision of Lao Tzu. Sage! Teach me your Way. Although the bustling hamlet lies quite far down the road, the clamor of chickens and calves penetrates the mist.

He turns his head and gives me a wink. He's not happy to be back; he's delighted.

Sage! Tell me your truths. Yes, I left home during the overcast season when the damsons bloomed, but what have I learned from living and doing? I surrendered my youth yet got nothing in return. Sage! Sun still beams high over country lanes where I hear the distant voices of village girls chanting as they weave. Sage! Why not speak to me about your Way? Why visit an illusory hamlet where peaches and damsons bloom? Is it because you search in silence for those abstruse principles of human consciousness that words cannot explain?

He slaps his hands together sharply, sits up and points a finger in the air. He talks with me like an old friend.

Yes, this man of moral force will visit that hamlet around

noon and sit down in some farmhouse kitchen but I shall not seek him out!

"You seek me out. Here you are, delighted to be back. We certainly don't seek out abstruse principles of human consciousness that words cannot explain. Exactly the opposite. We want to explain human consciousness, specifically to understand the workings of your mind. That doesn't sound abstruse to me."

He smiles, looks away, looks back and smiles again. He lies down.

Buddha. Riddle of the world. You who sleep in those forlorn grottoes adorning that hilly locale rich with reddish soil. You are not a shellfish, not bones, not matter, not a long-rusted clock in that sandy soil where plants wilt along the riverbank. Indeed, are you perhaps the shadow of *truth* or even a ghost? Oh, living mummy, your icons sit in those grottoes like wondrous fish—year after year after year after year!

I repeat, dragging out the words as he just had, "year after year after year after year." I ask, "Is such a living mummy an abstruse principle of human consciousness?"

I hear in the distance the rumbling surge of a gigantic tsunami. Eternal man, oh, Buddha, do you hear it, too?

"Cleaning out the grottoes of the mind, stuffed with thousands of icons for thousands of years, will take a force as gigantic as that of a tsunami. Even Buddha, that eternal man, will get washed out of human consciousness."

A huge sea turtle lies here like a hill, and a giant clam shell

of unimaginable thickness has a panoramic view of the locale near Paleozoic seas. Tell me, my love, how much longer shall we sit side by side on these somber rocks? Sun immeasurably distant, and yet wherever sunbeams shine one hears the riotous hum of conch shells.

"Whenever we sit side by side, as we are right now, we hear the riotous hum of us talking. True, our talking gets disrupted by illness. By saké. You name it. And it's certainly not eternal. But when sunbeams shine and life flows, ah, hear the riotous hum."

He feigns exasperation.

My dearest love, you know I'm already dispossessed of hope, nor have I the solace of a tranquil life! Whatever I do makes me maniacally depressed. What shall we do on this dreadfully isolated strand, my love? I tremble here like a chunk of some giant clam.

"From where I'm sitting, you're trembling with the happiness of someone returned from a grave illness. You tremble realizing how much you need to share your distress."

My passions have no way to vent, nor—oh, my love!—do you realize the gamut of my distress.

"How'd you put it? A huge turtle lies here like a hill and there's a clam shell of unimaginable thickness. And also love, dearest love, your love. That's me. Not eternal. Not even paleozoic. But returning here today is like summer. Happy days are here again!"

A sweetness hangs in the air. He looks at me, not knowing what to make of it all. I don't either, but I have no doubt it's wonderful. Conflict and hate are simpler to deal with.

Love and rapture simply *are*. They threaten a cognitive disconnect. How does one deal with pure being? I realize I'm humming *Lullaby and Goodnight*. It strikes me as lovely as a riotous hum in a conch shell.

Notes from Aboveground

In 1922 Sakutarô's second daughter was born. In mid-December of that year undefined intestinal problems confined him to bed. He then read the *Confucian Analects* and edited the manuscript of his second book of poetry, *Blue Cat*. This avidly awaited collection he published in January 1923.

I've packed my lunar almanac in the basket

The poet flees the modern world of the solar calendar. Reference to lunar time implies a pre-modern era and the sexual, psychic and unconscious dimensions associated with the moon. This almanac, a quaint guide for daily living, facilitates dream interpretation and forecasts auspicious dates for farming as well as family and business transactions.

Way of the True Disciple—From a vision of Lao Tzu

Lao Tzu, the legendary founder of Taoism, urged a "no sweat" attitude that lets life take its course. "Be like water," he advised, which finds its own level without thought—simply by doing "what comes naturally." Most Taoist principles run counter to the uptight, straight-laced, puritanical, and convention-touting Confucianism that dominated Japan during the poet's life. How committed is Sakutarô to "the path of virtue?" "His Horniness" preferred being enslaved to the weed and the pleasures of wine, women and song.

Buddha. Riddle of the world.
You who sleep in those forlorn grottoes

Buddha, like Lao Tzu, taught non-attachment and spiritual tranquillity. How could Sakutarô possibly achieve such virtues? Self-indulgence and preoccupation with adoration, not to mention alcohol, dominated his life. No icons of Lao Tzu populated those distant Chinese caves, which symbolize the womb and rebirth, or the unconscious. He finds Gautama the greater riddle. Caves warehousing the Buddha's countless statues represent eternal stasis. Critics believe Sakutarô refers to the forty grottoes at Yün-kang that date from the 5th century. Or he may refer to the Lung-men grottoes near Lo-yang that contain over 100,000 images of the Buddha ranging from a few inches to one that is five stories tall.

Hagiwara Sakutarô, Late 1930s

PART V

Groups

NOTES FROM UNDERGROUND

He comes in, jaw set. His mien suggests no nonsense.

Our Boss. Innately fearless, he boldly gave the signal with a stouthearted and astutely urgent look: "Go, boys! Go!"

"Make your mark, lads! A good papa urging on his kids."

In broad daylight they forced their way into a foreign firm and took by force a woman walking down the street. Their all but miraculous undertaking truly appeared to match the canons of civility. Since their dream-like violence was a calm, lightning quick operation, cars passed by oblivious to the deed.

"The exercise of force is compatible with the canons of

civility, so it must not take place in the physical world. The violence is dream-like. I suggest you're describing an upheaval of the mind."

Nodding vigorously he races on,

Not the slightest disturbance of the peace. Thanks to their canny schemes, their valor, their nonchalance, and their irrepressible passions, these inherently daring and dauntless fellows resemble birds slicing freely through the skies. Look! Look! The site of the mob's assault—illuminated by will and reason, the gangsters' secrets exposed and idols everywhere torn down.

"The other day you threatened the Buddha with a tsunami that would sweep away the idols. Aren't you that tsunami? You link Buddha with a gangster and identify religious idols as products of gangsterism. Surely such a blasphemous linkage will bring about an incalculable disturbance of the peace. In a lightning quick operation you intend to overthrow religion.

"Free will illuminated by reason is now the boss. By the exercise of these powers the boss claims his woman, Wisdom. You will wash away the familiar and the comforting. By what authority do you tear down idols that have endured thousands of years? What gives you the right to make yourself such a boss?

"You claim, 'Not the slightest disturbance of the peace.' I remind you of the question put to Jesus by the Pharisees. Jesus had performed miracles on the Sabbath, healing the sick. This violated the religious tradition of no work on the appointed day of rest. 'By what authority doest thou these things?' the Pharisees asked threateningly. Not even miracles justify violating religious canons."

I am cranked. Every muscle, ligament, blood vessel, my

belly and bowels, my vast acreage of skin throb with life, focused by the powerful lens of Hagiwara Sakutarô's mind.

He raises a fist. Arm outstretched, he gives a Nazi-type salute.

Our Boss!

His arm stays taut, untiring. Growling, he says,

Our Boss gives the signal with stouthearted and astutely urgent eyes. We are cowardly, scruffy and purposeless mobsters, but life throbs with consequence.

He builds to an enormous crescendo, finally screaming,

When we believe in our Boss!

"You think you're going to get away undermining such a grand fellow who makes life throb with consequence!" I holler back, "Have you lost your mind?"
He punches the air.

When we believe in our Boss, even the most despicable knave among us leaps directly into the fray, sword drawn.

Unsheathing his "weapon" and again at the top of his voice,

To battle the adversary in brawls over turf.

"Your boss makes for great soldiers, patriots, an aroused people. And here you go proposing will and reason as preferable! Are you serious?"

Like a hawk soaring through blue skies, our Boss is an independent man. By nature a dauntless and daring fellow, he plans, executes, predicts, works things out, has original ideas.

He jumps to his feet, raises both arms high over his head and shouts,

The Boss!

Then he collapses on the couch and doubles up with laughter. He straightens himself out and says dryly,

I associate commerce with flags. Consider the vessels that cross the seas of trade from far-off foreign lands! Note the exotic sailors who tramp through islands in the South Seas and Asia, possibly to load cotton and agate. As they sail to harbors where human liberty exists, flags of commerce flutter in various lands around the globe.

"I suggest you're also talking about commerce of the mind—from all harbors where human liberty exists allowing a free exchange of ideas."

Merchants! Dispatchers! Pilots! Don't you see the clouds now mounding densely before the dreadful gale? Don't you see the shapes of ghosts that toss and rage?

"New thoughts stir up the ghosts of tradition. These toss and rage against change."

Soon the masts will shatter, alarms will pierce the air, and then you'll see the pale fish of the ship floating belly-up.

"You went belly-up lately with Melancholia, ravaged by thinking unthinkable thoughts. You undermine your culture. You erode the beliefs of your people. You're Japanese. What's all this global business about? You and your people live on an island. You're fiercely proud of your traditions and beliefs."

Merchants: adventuresome freemen! Like a white cloud, you know these inscrutable, hard-to-resolve angsts. I associate commerce with flags.

"You associate thinking with international trading of ideas."
He snarls,

Seacow peasant! Grass sprouts from your farmhouse roof as your supper smoke drifts white in the sky.

"Stupid peasants, their minds a vegetative domain sprouting grass and not thoughts."

Thickset peasant, have you neglected your plowing? Famine threatens the countryside.

"Hear! Hear! Now what, great Adventurer! You claim the peasants are stupid seacows set in their ways. But without them, everybody starves. If you disturb them, how can they go about their work?"

Ancestral spirits shiver cheerlessly in the dim shadows your lamp casts over the family altar.

"Their religious beliefs provide them a sense of purpose and continuity and centeredness. The ancestral spirits give their lives meaning. And energy to do their hard and essential farming."

Brow wrinkled, he replies slowly,

Many Koreans had been killed, their spilled blood covering hundreds of acres. I look on, enraged at such atrocities!

"Parochialism instead of a global trading of ideas can have horrifying consequences, such as Japanese slaughtering thousands of Koreans. Bion linked this kind of phenomenon to Groupishness, a primitive and biologic given of the hominid brain. Groupishness enables folks to keep going, providing them a sense of purpose and a place in the scheme of things. Home Sweet Home."

Since his recovery from brain illness, Sakutarô and I have carried on our ZamaZama with immense energy and flair. Sheer aliveness. When he leaves the session, he stops at the door and looks back. He starts to say something, checks himself and vanishes.

Alas! I do not see him again for five years! I reflect, as the weeks pass and he never returns—nor drops a note to clarify his plans—that it is at this junction that the work so frequently ends, usually abruptly. Let race and religion come to life with the emotional vividness with which they slammed originally into our innards while we clung to mother's knee; it's over. What is astonishing is that without exception these "drop-outs" consider themselves free of racism and religious bigotry.

That's a harsh judgement. The fact remains that nothing human is more freighted with fantasy than sexual life and Group Life. True, Sakutarô has taken on sexuality at its most rivalrous, violent, envious level. He's marched us through Freud and the Oedipus complex, and then staggered through the primal depths of infantile fantasies and terrors. He intended to reveal the natural workings of his mind.

Well, I tell myself, ask Freud and Klein. I have no doubt they'd applaud his achievement. He did exactly that. Nonetheless, after all these exhausting efforts there remains the second great problem of human vulnerability, Group Life. Folks in every part of the world go along with their groups as mindlessly as the Japanese slaughtering the Koreans.

I'm disappointed. Surely Sakutarô of all people would find the courage to march on, taking us on the not-so-merry-go-round of religious and racial intolerance. No such luck. Like everyone else, he pulls up short. Goes so far and no further.

What's my evidence for these bitter pronouncements? My experience in institutes for psychoanalysis. Every psychoanalyst is required to undergo a personal analysis, three to five times a week, years on end. Yet the intellectual life of institutes is wracked interminably by what can only be described as religious wars. Freudians versus Kleinians versus Bionians versus whomever, wars every bit as primitive as Jonathan Swift's Big Endians slaughtering Little Endians, those rascals who insisted on breaking eggs on the little end. Blasphemy! I listened to Wilfred give a stunning and heuristic talk to an auditorium filled with psychoanalysts, entirely off the cuff, and they clapped him into silence, driving him off the podium. I observed this with my own eyes and ears.

Canons of civility? Not the slightest disturbance of the peace? Ha! Bion insisted psychoanalysis ignores religious life and the Groupishness underlying it. So does Sakutarô. He takes one last look and is gone. I expected better.

Notes from Aboveground

Our Boss.
Innately fearless, he boldly gave the signal

The English word "boss" doesn't suggest the nuances of the Japanese term, which implies a fatherly figure with vast authority and responsibility for the well-being of his mob, that is, his "children." The Japanese "boss" is at once the paterfamilias, a Mafia don and the patriarch. Sakutarô had a love-hate relationship with his high-achieving, demanding yet indulgent father. Usually, he found meek obedience to superiors an abomination.

Note the exotic sailors who tramp through islands
in the South Seas and Asia

Merchant captains stood near the top of Sakutarô's admiration list. He saw them as adventurous libertarians, passionately sailing uncharted waters, attempting the unattempted, hazarding failure. Dedicated to laissez-faire, these heroes overcame anxiety, loneliness and uncertainty to accomplish their missions—true individualists! How different from the run-of-the-mill, money-grubbing merchants he detested in Maebashi.

Thickset peasant, have you neglected your plowing

In Sakutarô's day, Japanese believed peasants shared facial shapes, body types, behaviors, values and attitudes. For centuries farmers intermarried only with nearby farmers, so their physical and psychological uniformity was remarkable.

Many Koreans had been killed

After the 1923 Kanto Earthquake, hysterical "patriots" sought scapegoats for the tragedy and massacred at least 3,000 Korean residents. Koreans, whom some regard Japan's invisible "Blacks," were seen as aliens. They're still discriminated against in schools and in the workplace.

Session
Cries of a Cosmic Waif

NOTES FROM UNDERGROUND

Sakutarô does not disappear from my life. From time to time he leaves a scrap of writing in the waiting room, obviously hand-delivered. The unstamped envelopes are invariably addressed, "Esteemed CP." It takes a while to figure out that stands for "Conversational Partner." I suspect he labels our relationship in this fashion more out of bitterness than jest. One spring he scribbles,

I'm inherently a nihilistic crow. Whatever the season, all I lack is everything.

A year later, these lines—so vivid I thought he was in the room talking to me:

Rural Clocks. In the country everyone lives with the ancestors. Old people, young people, housewives, children—the entire family lives under the same thatched

roof. They get up and go to bed before a venerable Buddhist altar adorned with the ancestors' sooted memorial tablets. Behind the home of every single farm exists a slightly elevated, winter-withered burial mound. The family's long history sleeps there with many bleached bones. Look! Ancient village shrines exactly as they were ages ago. Ancient white walls exactly as they were ages ago. Ancient natural landscapes exactly as they were ages ago. And villagers now make the same betrothals and marriage alliances the ancestors made in great-grandmother's distant past. Actually, country people know but a single unitary, eternal time that exists leisurely in a setting with no past, no present, no future. Change would mean ruin. Interrupting that time will unchain them from the reality in which they eternally exist. Since they desire proximity to their forebears, they desperately want to remain on the land. That's because once they leave the land, they'll have no abode to identify as their "native place." All births, weddings, and funerals take place within village walls, within the partitioned time and space of the rural milieu.

Early one Saturday at the local coffee emporium, as is my custom, I'm drinking Coffee of the Day, medium, room for cream, and reading the paper. While turning a page, I glimpse Sakutarô sitting across the table. I'm as startled as Stanley bumping into Livingston. "Mr. Hagiwara, I presume."

He bows. He looks all right. Thinner, perhaps, and of course, older, but his eyes are clear and shine with their accustomed intelligence. No evidence of the ravages of alcohol. His suit coat is threadbare, his cravat neatly tied under his chin.

"No coffee?"

He rolls his eyes and says,

Supper in an empty house.

"I'm not following."
He leans across the table and whispers,

I had supper with my family under yellow lamplight. No vegetables, no meat, no fish—only tasteless, leftover rice. That meal in our vacant home on the night of our move.

"What move?"

1929. Disowning my wife, I take my two children to Maebashi. The day I returned to Maebashi, my train lunged through violent winds. Awake, I sat alone by the window, the whistle shrieking through gloom and sparks illuminating the plain. Under shadows cast by the night train's dimmed lamps, my motherless children whimpered in their sleep. Truly aged, no place that welcomes me, wife and children scattered—isolated.

He moves forward. He speaks so low I cup an ear.

If you've come to see people off on their journeys, listen to me: clench your teeth to keep the pain of separation from shredding you!

"I'm sorry to hear you lost your family."

How can you return home without a home to go to—a place where someone might tenderly embrace and kiss you? Never having loved anything, nothing will ever love you.

The light from his eyes blinks off.

Fathers are everlastingly pathetic.

He shifts his gaze and begins chanting his words in sing-song fashion,

As he slept, he heard the pathetic sobbing of his child.
"Everyone's teasing me. They say I'm stupid."
The child was, in fact, an imbecile. Not only that, she had no mother.
"Don't cry. You're not stupid. You've just had bad luck. You're an unfortunate, ill-starred, pitiful child."
"What does 'ill-starred' mean, Daddy?"
"I'm talking about blunders."
"Blunders...?"
"Everything that people do without thought. For example, look! The fact that we were born, that we live, that we eat, that we marry, that we have children. Whatever, everything's a blunder."
"Is it okay if you think about it?"
"Even if you think about it, it's surely the same. It's a blunder."
"Then what can I do?"
"I don't know. Try asking Jesus."

He sits back and gives a deep sigh.

Fathers are everlastingly pathetic. In essence I'm a good-for-nothing man. In essence these are good-for-nothing books.

Only then do I notice the thin volumes on the table.

I'm going to sell them for a sen apiece.

"May I?" I ask, gesturing toward the volumes. His eyes light up, and he breaks unexpectedly into a broad smile. My face conveys a sense of confusion. Instantly he assumes a serious mien, nods his head vigorously, and in all earnestness, hands me a volume. It's in Japanese. We both burst out laughing, a moment as warm as the coffee.

I glance around the patio. The morning air is biting, a few scattered coffee drinkers inside. We are alone but not guaranteed privacy. However, small talk strikes me as a loss of nerve.

"Well," I say happily. "I have just the book for us—Oswald Spengler. Wouldn't you agree he's exactly the sort of fellow to bring up in a coffee house?

Sakutarô's eyes cloud over. Now he's confused.

"I thought perhaps you'd know of him. Spengler clarified why nihilistic crows lack everything, whereas villagers who live with their ancestors have everything."

Then I realize my mistake. Sakutarô and I are conversing in the 1920s. Spengler's famous book, *The Decline of the West*, isn't coming out for another decade.

"Time travel isn't as easy as it sounds. It's sort of like lying —I'm always covering my tracks," I explain to Sakutarô. He smiles and the light returns to his eyes.

I gather up a fresh head of steam.

"Spengler will say that villagers and that crow of yours live in separate worlds, derived from entirely different mathematical assumptions. Villagers are Euclidean. Euclid you've heard of. He's been around a couple thousand years and spelled out the geometric world. Reality is what we see, always a measurable magnitude.

"We all experience that kind of space for the first time snuggling in the arms of our mother. It is based on a deep need for visible boundaries. For years we remain in eye contact with her, and she with us. When a village infant nurses at the breast, it is framed by the light of its mother's face, filling the void. It lies against the mother's body, its original home. Home is forever a place, as reassuring as the milk splashing around in its tummy."

Sakutarô responds bitterly,

Unable to bear my thirsts, I staggered to the Reeling Moon and opened the door. The clamor of a cracked record echoed from that rowdy dive. There, under a sooty lamp on town's edge, I lined up a scanty row of saké bottles.

A couple, each carrying a coffee container, comes outside. They glance at us, having picked up Sakutarô's tone, hesitate and then move on down the street. I decide there is no turning back. Here in this egalitarian setting—no couch, no degrees, no psychoanalytic fathers!—I will allow myself to initiate ideas.

I say, "Try asking Jesus about thirst. One of his seven words on the cross: 'I thirst.' Astonishing. Thirst overrides the agonies of a crucifixion. I suggest that means, 'Mother, I thirst!' Body is forever thirsty, forever hungry, forever in need of a holy place where it can be held and cared for.

"Spengler will point out that the number three is the 'holy number' and is corporeal. It denotes sexual union and its product, propagation. Euclidean space houses a village in which arithmetic also becomes corporeal—mama and papa and baby make three."

Last year I stayed in a sepulchral Western-style room, a fifth-floor apartment where I slept alone on a bed shoved against the wall. Visitors knocked at my door, witnessed my apathy, and left pitying me.

"A Western-style room liberates you from conventions of your Japanese past. From the village of your origin." I pounded on the slim volumes in front of him. "Each of us is born into a village, and we remain villagers forever. We are born and live and eat and marry and have children in a village. Unless we live our lives within a palpable geometry and a corporeal arithmetic, we find ourselves lost. We've always been villagers. Traversing backwards across ages too long to count, we'll see our ancestral bones transmogrify into the bones of huddled apes."

Yet with neither coal nor a stove in that chalk-walled, sepulchral Western room, I lay abed sobering up.

"Cut off from your roots, you are left without energy, apathetic, alone in a sepulchral world. You want to find Euclid. 'Where on earth am I?' And next ask him, 'Which way to my village, Maebashi?' Home, that dearest freshness, energizes each of us to go on."

He drinks his coffee, now cooled, in great gulps.

When I calmly canvas my inner self, I'm astonished at how unfulfilled I feel.

I nod in vigorous agreement. "You describe yourself as inherently a nihilistic crow. Well, that bird couldn't find a cherry tree in full bloom in the middle of Maebashi. He lacks everything. That bird has nothing—that is, no-thing. What is there about no-thing to crow about? The villager lives in a plenum, space filled as completely as the belly of a well-nursed infant. All Euclidean geometry, corporeal arithmetic."

I'm inherently a nihilistic crow.

"You wrote me that one spring."

On the first day of winter I open my beak and clamor like a weathervane on a high roof. Whatever the season, all I lack is everything.

"Mr. Crow embraces a different mathematics. He commits the sacrilege of disclosing the irrational—for example, the employment of unending decimal fractions such as pi. Nihilistic Mr. Crow tumbles into infinity, where the infinite spaces terrify."

While smoke hazes the sky, I fail again to come across a position I can hold.

"Here is Spengler's great insight. The symbol of the West is an idea of which no other culture gives even a hint, the idea of function. Function is complete emancipation from any pre-existent idea of number, and Euclidean geometry ceases to have any value. A function merely connects two points, creating a thing which is virtualized out of infinite space. We have gone from a closed world to an infinite universe. There is no fixed position. There is no center. Every position is as indeterminate as smoke hazing the sky."

Sakutarô snaps his fingers, his face blazing forth Eureka! He speaks slowly, savoring his words.

For some time a starved octopus had been housed in an aquarium tank. Light entering through the frosted ceiling glass loitered ceaselessly somber behind the dreary shadow of a rock below. Having long figured that the octopus was dead, everyone had disremembered this dismal container. Only stale saltwater remained in the glassed-in tank bathed by dust-laden sunbeams. The octopus had

not died but had taken shelter behind the rock. Day after day whenever he awoke, the octopus in this miserable deserted tank had to endure fierce pangs of hunger. When nobody fed him and he had run out of food, he began to eat his tentacles. First one, then another. At last, when all his tentacles were gone, he inverted his insides and began eating them. Little by little. One morsel after another. Systematically.

My eyes grow wide as saucers.
He cranes his face forward, now radiant, transfigured.

Thus did the octopus consume his entire self: here and there—from his skin to his brain to his stomach—till nothing remained. Completely gone.

He brings his hands to my face, almost touching me.

Gone but not dead,

he shouts out, startling me and an old codger who is working a crossword puzzle at a nearby table.

I feel a sudden, deep affection for Sakutarô. He comes across so frail and yet so plucky, braced against the tsunami of deep time and the terrifying infinite spaces.

I gather up courage. "I love your plucky octopus. When he realizes his three-dimensional, bounded, watery world is disappearing right in front of him—he had always figured it was as enduring as the very seas—he rethinks the whole business."

Even after he had disappeared, the octopus still existed enduringly through several centuries, this creature, with his appalling deficiencies and discontentment, had been alive, though invisible to the human eye.

"What happens to his body? What happens to his filled-to-the-top world? What happens to Octopus Plenum? Gone. Emptied. Yet he manages to cut out a place for himself that by no stretch of the imagination can be thought of.... Wait!"

I slap the table in delight. "Precisely by stretching his imagination he creates a no-place and hangs on for dear life! Maybe for several centuries. What kind of time is several centuries? Not something a rural clock ticks off. Tick-tock, tick-tock, one-two, one-two. Those are integral and corporeal numbers."

Sakutarô puts his hands together and makes an ironic little bow.

Look! Ancient village shrines exactly as they were ages ago. Ancient white walls exactly as they were ages ago. Ancient natural landscapes exactly as they were ages ago. And villagers now make the same betrothals and marriage alliances the ancestors made in great-grandmother's distant past.

"Let's see. Great-great-grandmother lived to ninety. Grandmother lived to eighty-one, but grandfather lived only to sixty-one. They're all there, in that slightly elevated burial mound. 'The family's long history sleeps with many bleached bones.'"

Sakutarô laughs as I intone slowly his own words. I hurry on.

"Bones have magnitude and number. One can count them on fingers and toes. By contrast, several centuries sound as indefinite as pi.

"Actually, country people know but a single unitary, eternal time that exists leisurely in a setting with no past, no present, no future."

I sit back. This is hard work. Especially for a Saturday morning when the spirit is willing but the flesh is weak. I stand up. "I'll get us two coffees. Cream and sugar?"

He nods yes.

"That's how I like it, too. Cream to the very top."

He smiles wryly. When I return, Sakutarô has scarcely moved.

I plunge right back into our ZamaZama before even sitting down. "Bion would love your octopus. By the way, Bion is the only genius I ever knew personally."

Sakutarô arches his eyebrows.

"OK, you're the second," I say, putting his coffee down in front of him. "Bion would say your octopus suffered a thought. 'Hey, what gives? My plenum isn't full of plenty. It's missing stuff!' And what caused the octopus to have this thought and to know something's missing? Pain. 'Fierce pangs of hunger,' as you put it."

Sakutarô stops blowing on his hot coffee, all ears.

"Here's Bion's genius. Pain evoked by something missing can give rise to thinking. Bion observed that what's missing is a No-Thing—there's nothing in the octopus's belly! That nothing, however, registers as a Bad Thing! Can't do anything with it except get rid of it. Fill plenum with good things and, presto! the bad things are gotten rid of. We'll call this exchange the Euclidean three-dimensional shuffle."

I wiggle my shoulders in a clumsy dance. Sakutarô bursts out laughing, spraying coffee on his lap.

I chuckle, too. "Isn't that the full-time occupation of your villagers? Preserve the plenum? Make sure nothing's missing? Like Jesus, they want the place the same yesterday, today and forever. Not so for your poor octopus. He gives it his best shot, no doubt, inverting his insides, gobbling up every bit of skin and brain and stomach, until nothing's left of a three-dimensional world. What is your octopus to do?

Here's where *your* genius comes in."

Sakutarô answers instantly,

Even after he had disappeared, the octopus still existed enduringly in that place.

"Exactly! What else is that place but the place of Mind? Bion would say your plucky octopus created genuine thoughts—alpha elements linked through alpha-function—and from these creations he could generate meaning in non-Euclidean space. He had passed from a closed world to an infinite universe. He had turned himself inside out on his way to becoming a thinking animal."

For a few minutes, we drink our coffee in silence. I look around the patio. The old codger has left, and we are again alone.

Sakutarô frowns and leans forward. He whispers sadly,

Once they leave the land, they'll have no abode to identify as their "native place." Interrupting that time will unchain them from the reality in which they eternally exist.

I hesitate, then say, "That's why I'm truly sad to hear you lost your wife and children. Freud observed, 'The ego is first and foremost a body ego.' He recognized that we are first and foremost and forever biology. We are born, we live, we eat, we marry, we have children. These experiences give rise to problems; these are what our initial conversations investigated. Surely it's a blunder to live biologic life without such investigation."

Since they desire proximity to their forebears, they desperately want to remain on the land.

"Don't villagers dance hand in hand with Euclid, visibly bounded by venerable Buddhist altars and ancestors' memorial tablets?"

Abruptly Sakutarô gets up and walks through the patio to the curb. He stares at the street for several minutes. Then, to my relief, turns around and marches back to our table.

Standing over me he barks,

Try asking Jesus!

I am caught off-guard by his hostility—until I reflect on how much time and energy this man from the Orient has given to the study of Occidental religion. I grasp he is trying to connect two points—venerable Buddhist altars and Jesus. Spengler's function. When he once more sits down, I say tentatively, "Jesus is scary. He isn't your octopus."

I continue to think and mull. Sakutarô doesn't take his eyes off me, but I feel no pressure. I sense a thought building. Slowly the bits and pieces drifting into awareness begin to cohere. I spread out my palms and start linking each word carefully with the next.

"In the beginning was the Word. The beginning of what? I assume Mind. Mind began with the invention of human language, so mind began with the Word, when flesh and everything else got represented by words. What I find scary about Jesus is that with him the Word became flesh. That's turning the story around. It now goes backwards. Your octopus went from flesh to thought. The Incarnation—the central dogma of Christianity—reverses this development. The word becomes flesh, that is, local and bound and as ingestible as the bread and wine of the Eucharist. God becomes Euclidean."

I take a swallow of coffee. Our eyes meet, a moment of tenderness as the cream and sugar and coffee swill and flow warmly down. "Groups, villages, religions forever turn the story backwards. Their traditions and gods become things-in-themselves, useless for taking thought, for moving the story forward. In your village every nook and cranny is filled with routine and tradition and certitude, as useless for thinking as a burial mound filled with bones. Time can't flow in such a place. It's in a closed container. No room for human growth and development."

Sakutarô leans back and stretches. He smiles wanly.

I wrote a letter home on a counter in the post office. Shoes and fate worn thin, I'm the ruin of a crow.

It occurs to me I am with a great human being. He did not drop out. These past five years he wore himself thin, a nihilistic crow, flying in the face of gods and the unexamined group terrors that create them.

It's May now. Time to refurbish the way we look at human awareness. To liberate ourselves from conventions of the past, from unreasonable moralities, from utterly obsolescent truths, from society's silly mores.

He has stayed the course. He has learned to think.

He gets up, brushes his thinning hair back from his temple and takes a deep resolved breath. He looks at me for a moment, turns and walks briskly into the city. He disremembers his thin volumes of poems. I slip them into my jacket.

I never see him again.

Notes from Aboveground

I'm inherently a nihilistic crow

The original title of this poem was, "Negate Everything!" That, Sakutarô thought, was the basic attitude of the crow, which the Japanese see as the messenger of death. Exacting revenge by rejecting every conventional value, the crow served both as his metaphor of rebellion against society and as a primary figure of alienation.

Supper in an empty house

Sakutarô published this work in March 1928. As he had not recently moved, it is possible that he may refer to 1925 events: either to his February relocation from Maebashi to Ôi Machi in Tokyo or to his November move to Kamakura for wife Ineko's health. At the time of that move he complained that his desk and other baggage were late in arriving.

Disowning my wife, I took my two children to Maebashi

These words come from the subtitle of the poem, "Homecoming." Sakutarô had by parental arrangement married Ineko in May 1919. The marriage lasted ten years. Ineko soon realized she was competing with the ghost of Elena. Three years after moving to Tokyo, Ineko became more interested in dancing and "having fun" than in caring for her family. In 1929, when she was thirty, she ran off with a man considerably younger than Sakutarô, then forty-three. Sakutarô said his split with Ineko made him feel unworthy. He knew Ineko realized she competed with Elena. Their parting was one of the most painful events of his life. He returned with his daughters to Maebashi in June of 1929 but set the poem in winter to emphasize his wretchedness. Once home, he learned his father was gravely ill.

The child was, in fact, an imbecile

Sakutarô's second daughter, Akirako, born in 1922, experienced a severe fever as a child and suffered brain damage. The family was convinced her handicap resulted from Ineko's neglect of her children. Akirako eventually required institutionalization. Most people then regarded "damaged" children as retribution for bad karma and shamefully concealed them.

Last year I stayed in a sepulchral Western-style room

For most of his adult life Sakutarô preferred Western clothing and sleeping arrangements.

A fifth-floor apartment where I slept alone

Actually, Sakutarô stayed in room #28 of the two-story Nogizaka Club Apartments. Five stories both suggests the ultimate height for a 1931 structure in Tokyo and increases the poet's sense of estrangement. Could he have known that since the number five has an erotic dimension it symbolizes the burgeoning of spring and the fullness of life?

I fail again to come across a position I can hold

The truth is, he wasn't even looking, though his father always hoped he was.

For some time a starved octopus had been housed in an aquarium tank

The octopus doesn't exist in its natural state but is confined to a small tank. Stasis and restriction Sakutarô regarded as extreme and unusual punishment; the octopus, meant to live freely in the sea, destroys itself in captivity. With an animistic touch, it lives eternally as a "spirit." Sakutarô said this work intends to ask, "What is life? What is death?"

I wrote a letter home on a counter in the post office

This doubtless refers to a slapdash acknowledgment of his dole. Certainly he cannot be writing a long or detailed note. Because Sakutarô always described post offices as bursting with people, he may well be holding up the line and inconveniencing patrons.

It's May now. Time to refurbish the way we look at human awareness

Sakutarô had been a citizen of Tokyo for some sixteen months when this poem appeared. The revolutionary anti-convention and anti-family stance of this slight work would not shock people in the capital; they were accustomed to intellectual palaver and could let it go in one ear and out the other. These remarks would raise hackles in Maebashi.

Afterword

Freud said of his job, "No one who, like me, conjures up the most evil of those half-tamed demons that inhabit the human breast, and seeks to wrestle with them, can expect to come through the struggle unscathed."

Artists, like Scientific Conversationalists, haul us into their inner world. Any serious attempt to comprehend their stuff calls for a deep—and risky!—level of engagement. For example, precisely because Sakutarô was a great poet, his melancholic self-loathing and depressions become our own. We salute your courage for having taken him on. Like Freud—like us!—we're sure you didn't come through unscathed.

CHRONOLOGY

1886 November 1: Born in Maebashi, capital of Gunma Prefecture, some 69 miles north of Tokyo. He was the first son of Dr. Mitsuzô (1852-1930), the third son of a family of hereditary physicians in Ôsaka, and Kei (1867-1951), the first daughter of a prominent Maebashi samurai family.

1890 April: Enters the kindergarten of the Prefectural Normal School. Sickly, Sakutarô misses many classes. Shows an uncommon early love for music.

1892 May: Cousin Eiji (1878–1936) from the main family in Ôsaka stays with the Hagiwara family to attend high school in Maebashi. A Christian, Eiji interests Sakutarô in reading the Bible and exerts a significant influence on him.

1893 April: Enters first grade in the elementary school attached to the Prefectural Normal School, a five or six minute walk from home. Sakutarô loves to read anything, especially books like *Alice in Wonderland*. Enjoys writing; soon begins submitting stories to youth magazines.
1900 March: Enters the prefectural high school. Magic and card games fascinate him; enjoys playing harmonica and concertina. Interest in literature begins his second year.

1902 December: Publishes five tanka, traditional thirty-one syllable poems. Sakutarô shows interest in free verse and drawing. Obsessed with photography and his darkroom. Actively involved in leading a literary club at school.

1903 May: Publishes four tanka in a Tokyo youth magazine. July: Three tanka appear in a major journal. Success encourages him to submit verse to other central magazines. Writes nearly 250 tanka by graduation. Gets his mother to buy him a mandolin.

1904 April: Excessive cutting of classes forces him to repeat the fifth year of high school. Places tanka in local and national publications. Fall: Attracted to sister Waka's friend Baba Nakako (1890–1917), the first daughter of a nearby pharmaceutical wholesaler. She's the Elena, her

1914 baptismal name, who appears in many early poems.

1906 March: Graduates from high school, prepares for college entrance exams.

1907 April: Fails the exam to an Ôsaka medical school. Qualifies for Fifth College in Kumamoto. September: Enters as an English literature major.

1908 July: Fails the first year at Kumamoto. Takes and passes the exam to Sixth College in Okayama. September: Transfers to Okayama, where he switches his major from English to German literature and law.

1909 July: Crazy about ping-pong. Cuts so many classes he must repeat the first year.

1910 April: Enters then drops out of the Keiô College preparatory school in Tokyo. Father still hopes Sakutarô might become a doctor. July: Sakutarô contracts typhus at Okayama and drops out of school. November: Ôsaka cousin Eiji returns to Maebashi to intern at the Hagiwara Hospital.

1911 January: Goes to Tokyo to study the mandolin with well-known teachers, Japanese and Italian. May: Once again enters the Keiô preparatory course. November: Drops out of Keiô for "family reasons." In Tokyo, Sakutarô attends many modern plays and operas. Also considers entering the Ueno Conservatory of Music. He wisely fears, however, he could never pass the theory and history areas of the entrance exam.

1912 June: Studies guitar with a teacher in Tokyo. December: Cousin Eiji leaves Maebashi to engage in medical research in Tokyo.

1913 May: Publishes five modern poems, including "Night Train," regarded a masterpiece. The editor urges Sakutarô to give up tanka and concentrate instead on free verse.

1914 January: Sakutarô's mandolin band begins to perform concerts in and around Maebashi. Father has a shed behind the hospital converted into Sakutarô's Western-style study-bedroom. A British magazine provides models for his self-designed clothing. Maebashi townsmen consider him an unfilial wastrel and a dandy; his outlandish accoutrements and behavior enhance his bohemian playboy image.

1917 February: With money that mother Kei gets from Mitsuzô, Sakutarô self-publishes his first collection of free verse, *Howling at the Moon*. The language, content, and imagery of this volume cause a sensation among most Tokyo literary circles and bring instant renown, as Sakutarô had predicted. May 5: Elena dies of tuberculosis.

1919 May 1: Marries Ueda Ineko (born 1899). The couple lives with Sakutarô's parents.

1920 September 4: First daughter Yôko born. She becomes a dancer and writer.

1922 May: Reissues *Howling at the Moon*. September 1: Daughter Akirako born. Early brain damage eventually necessitates her institutionalization.

1923 January: Publishes his second collection, *Blue Cat* ("blue" = the English sense of "sad;" cat = tomcat seeking sex). July: Issues his third free-verse collection, *Dreaming Butterflies*. These three volumes establish Sakutarô as a leading modern poet.

1925 February: Father will support him, so he moves to Tokyo with wife and daughters. Rents a flat in a plebeian neighborhood by the railroad yards in Ôi Machi. April: Sickened by polluted air, the family flees to the suburbs. August: Issues his fourth collection, *Pure Lyrics*. November: Ineko's bad health forces a move to Kamakura.

1926 Late November: Relocates from a Kamakura beach house to another Tokyo suburb.

1928 February: Publishes *Poetry: Theory and Impressions*. March: Issues an anthology containing twenty-one new poems. December: Publishes *Principles of Poetry*. Problems with Ineko increase. After becoming involved in ballroom dancing, she gets interested in and starts dating younger men and neglects her daughters.

1929 June: Ineko runs off to Hokkaido with a younger, more "compatible" man. July: Sakutarô takes his daughters back to Maebashi. October: Publishes a collection of aphorisms titled *The*

Justice of Delusions. Officially divorces Ineko.

1930 July 1: Father dies at age seventy-seven. Sakutarô inherits, but mother Kei controls both income and the Hagiwara register. October: The family moves to Tokyo and rents a house.

1933 January: The two-story home that Sakutarô helped design is completed in Setagaya Ward. Moves in with mother, sister Ai (born 1904), and his two daughters.

1934 June: Issues *Isle of Ice* (his title: *The Iceland* [= Japan]), his last book of new verse.

1936 March: Publishes *Authentic Blue Cat*, a collection of earlier free verse.

1937 December: Joins the Tokyo Amateur Magician's Club.

1938 Late April: Marries Ôtani Mitsuko, a twenty-seven-year-old woman who delights in his guitar and mandolin serenades. They honeymoon until summer's end.

1939 February: Mother Kei refuses to register their union, drives Mitsuko away.
1940 July: Issues *Prodigal*, a collection of essays on poetry. July: Issues the aphorism collection *In Port*. October: Publishes *Imbecile*, miscellaneous impressions and comments, mainly on poetry. November 11–15: Sick in bed with a cold. December: *Prodigal* receives a literary prize for the best work published during 1940.

1941 Mid-August: Goes to Maebashi to deliver a lecture. Catches a severe cold.

1942 May 11: Dies at 55. Pneumonia listed officially as the cause of death, but Sakutarô's symptoms suggest he may have suffered from lung cancer. Interred in Maebashi.

INDEX OF POEMS CITED

Verses cited are from *Rats' Nests: The Poetry of Hagiwara Sakutarô*, translated by Robert Epp, Second Edition, Revised and Expanded (Paris: UNESCO Publishing 1999).

ABOUT THE AUTHOR

Frederick Kurth, M.D., graduated from Indiana University School of Medicine, 1955.

He spent three years as a primary care physician in the bayou country of Louisiana, serving as assistant coroner. He owned and operated a twelve-bed hospital during his years as a country doctor.

Dr. Kurth completed a three-year residency program in psychiatry, spending two years at Louisiana State University in New Orleans, the third at Cedars-Sinai in Los Angeles. He graduated from the Los Angeles Psychoanalytic Institute/Society in 1966. He practiced psychoanalysis in Beverly Hills for twenty years, then both psychoanalysis and psychiatry in Hawthorne and Huntington Beach. He continues in full-time practice.

His publications include "The Structuring Aspects of the Penis," in *The International Journal of Psychoanalysis*; "Projective Identification" in *The Psychoanalytic Forum*; "Bion's Grid." in *Do I Dare Disturb the Universe? Collected Essays in Honor of Wilfred Bion*.